A TIME FOR MARTYRS: THE LIFE OF

MALCOLM X

A TIME FOR MARTYRS: THE LIFE OF

MALCOLM X

DAVID ARETHA

MORGAN REYNOLDS PUBLISHING

Greensboro, North Carolina

The U.S. Constitution

CIVIL RIGHTS LEADERS

A Time for Martyrs: The Life of Malcolm X

Copyright © 2013 by Morgan Reynolds Publishing

Library of Congress Cataloging-in-Publication Data

Aretha, David.
A time for martyrs : the life of Malcolm X / by David Aretha.
p. cm. -- (Civil rights leaders)
Includes bibliographical references and index.
ISBN 978-1-59935-328-9 -- ISBN 978-1-59935-329-6 (e-book)
1. X, Malcolm, 1925-1965--Juvenile literature. 2. Black
Muslims--Biography--Juvenile literature. 3. African
Americans--Biography--Juvenile literature. I. Title.
BP223.Z8L57165 2012
320.54'6092--dc23
[B]

2011048171

Printed in the United States of America
First Edition

Book cover and interior designed by:
Ed Morgan
navyblue design studio
Greensboro, NC

Malcolm X holding up a newspaper while addressing African American Muslims at a New York City rally in 1963

Malcolm X praying in a mosque on July 10, 1964

CONTENTS

Malcolm X addressing the
topic of desegregation in
Harlem in May, 1963

1 "WHO TAUGHT YOU TO HATE YOURSELF?"

ON MAY 22, 1962, MALCOLM X looked out upon hundreds of well-dressed black Americans in a large room in Los Angeles, California. Camera crews were there too, prepared to cover the most polarizing man in America. While other black leaders, such as Martin Luther King Jr., were careful not to fully antagonize white Americans, Malcolm X was never afraid to call it like he saw it.

In this speech, the topic was hate. White Americans had accused Malcolm's religious organization, the Nation of Islam (NOI) led by Elijah Muhammad, of preaching hatred of white people. The NOI, believing that whites had oppressed blacks throughout world history, opposed integration. They proposed a separate black nation, where American-born blacks could finally shed their shackles and determine their own destiny.

Was that hate? Not to Malcolm. In his mind, the more salient point was that white America—through racist systems, words, and tone—had made black Americans hate themselves.

Dressed dapperly in a dark suit and black-rimmed glasses, the tall, slender, clean-cut preacher stood arrow-straight. He spoke forcefully with a throaty voice.

"Who taught you to hate the texture of your hair?" he asked his black audience. Touching his cheeks with both hands, he asked, "Who taught you to hate the color of your skin to such an extent that you *bleach* to get like the white man? Who taught you to hate the shape of your nose and the shape of your lips?" Malcolm, a onetime boxer, punched the air for emphasis, determined to drive home his point. "Who taught you to hate *yourself* from the top of your head to the soles of your feet?"

Those in attendance hung on his every word, nodding their support and calling back with "mm-hmm" and "that's right."

"Who taught you to hate your own kind?" Malcolm continued. "Who taught you to hate the race that you belong to, so *much* so that you don't want to be around each other? Before you come asking Mr. Muhammad does he teach hate, you should ask yourself, Who taught you to hate being what God gave you?"

The audience erupted in applause, but Malcolm had more to say. This, after all, was the beginning of a black revolution, and Malcolm X was at the vanguard. The civil rights movement, which had begun in 1955 with the Montgomery bus boycott in Alabama, had inspired black Americans to stand up for their rights. Malcolm wasn't part of that movement; he didn't just quietly take a seat at a segregated lunch counter, hoping for a cup of coffee. At the top of his lungs, he was chastising white America for three centuries' worth of racial oppression.

Malcolm had spent time in prison for larceny and breaking and entering. But on this day in Los Angeles, he rebuffed the criticism that he and others in the Nation of Islam had criminal records. "You cannot be a Negro in America and not have a criminal record," he said as the crowd burst into

A police officer in Montgomery, Alabama, gets fingerprints from Rosa Parks.

applause. "Martin Luther King has been to jail. James Farmer has been to jail. You can't name a black man in this country who is sick and tired of the hell that he's catching who hasn't been to jail."

"They put *Moses* in jail," he continued with a slash of his hand. "They put *Daniel* in jail. Why, you haven't got a man of God in the Bible that wasn't put in jail when they started speaking up against exploitation and oppression."

Amid heavy applause, Malcolm wiped his brow and then got back to work. "They charged Jesus with sedition," he said. "Didn't they do that?" "Yes!" the crowd replied. "They said he was against Caesar," he said. "They said he was discriminating because he told his disciples, 'Go not the way of the Gentiles, but rather go to the lost sheep. . . . Go to the oppressed. Go to the downtrodden. Go to the exploited. Go to the people

13

who don't know who they are, who are lost from the knowledge of themselves and are strangers in a land that is not theirs.'"

The excitement in the crowd began to swell. "Go to *those* people," he said. "Go to the slaves. Go to the second-class citizens. Go to the ones who are suffering the brunt of Caesar's brutality. And if Jesus were here in America today, he wouldn't be going to the white man. The white man is the *oppressor*. He would be going to the oppressed. He would be going to the humble. He would be going to the lowly. He would be going to the rejected and the despised. He would be going to the so-called American Negro."

And with that, the audience erupted in powerful applause.

In his short, tumultuous life, Malcolm X would help bring the Nation of Islam into America's consciousness. During his years with the Nation and after he left the NOI in 1964, he led many black Americans on a different road to freedom than that provided by Martin Luther King Jr. MLK led a nonviolent movement, one in which demonstrators half-tried to get arrested or even beaten by police in order to generate sympathy from the white majority.

Martin Luther King Jr., arm in arm with his chief aide, Reverend Ralph Abernathy, as they begin the Selma to Montgomery march

Malcolm mocked King's tactics and philosophy. He equated his approach with being defenseless, and he called King a "fool" and a modern-day "Uncle Tom." No proud black person should allow himself or herself to be mentally, physically, and economically abused, Malcolm preached.

"I feel that when the law fails to protect Negroes from whites' attack, then those Negroes should use arms, if necessary, to defend themselves . . . ," he asserted. "I am speaking against and my fight is against the white *racists*. I firmly believe that Negroes have the right to fight against these racists, by any means that are necessary."

This insightful, charismatic preacher convinced young black Americans to take pride in their race and themselves. Malcolm, who once was told by his white teacher to forget about being a lawyer because "that's no realistic goal for a nigger," rejected half-measures. Instead, he inspired blacks to blast through societal constraints and be *full* men and women.

After his death, Malcolm's impact only intensified. *The Autobiography of Malcolm X*, published posthumously in 1965, sold 6 million copies by 1977 and was hailed by *Time* magazine as one of the ten most influential nonfiction books of the twentieth century. Malcolm's words inspired the leaders of the fledgling Black Power movement, which contributed to the race riots of the late 1960s but also inspired widespread black pride for the first time in the nation's history. Malcolm's legacy did not diminish but instead expanded as the decades passed. The Spike Lee film *Malcolm X* (1992) reinvigorated interest in the man and his message.

Historians are conflicted about whether or not Malcolm X had a positive influence. Critics say that his message was too angry, that he overly condemned the civil rights movement, and that his denunciation of white Americans was unfair to the righteous. Nevertheless, he was and is a hero to millions of black Americans as well as to others who despise racial injustice. In his time, he was a courageous cultural warrior, able to articulate the conflicted feelings of his people and fearlessly proclaim them to the world.

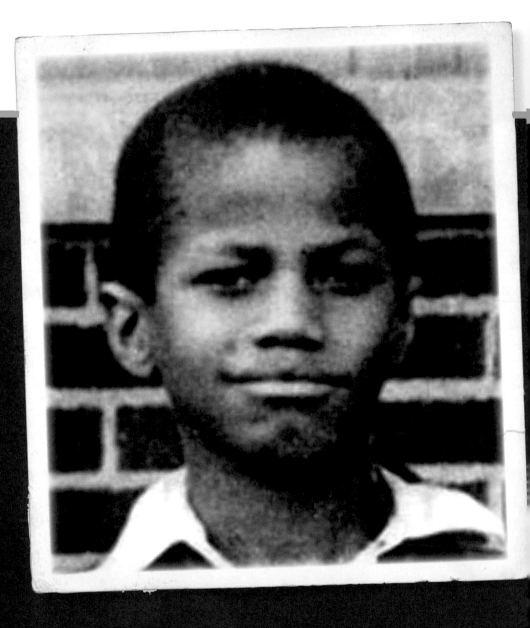

Young Malcolm Little, the boy who
would later be known as Malcolm X

2 BLACK CHILD IN A WHITE WORLD

ACCORDING TO MALCOLM, he experienced his first act of racism while he was still in his mother's womb.

One night in 1925—the heyday of the Ku Klux Klan—a group of Klansmen rode their horses to the Little house in Omaha, Nebraska. Louise Little, mother of three and pregnant with Malcolm, opened the door. As Malcolm recounted in his autobiography, the men wore hoods, carried torches, and brandished rifles and shotguns. They were looking for Louise's husband, Earl Little.

When Louise told them that he wasn't home, they responded with threats. The Klansmen demanded that the Littles move out of town, for they would not tolerate Earl's racial rhetoric. Earl Little had been preaching the message of Marcus Garvey: that there was no future for black Americans in the white-dominated United States; that they should move to Africa.

Showing that they meant business, the Klansmen rode around the house, shattering every windowpane with the butts of their guns. Then they rode off, torches blazing.

This would not be the worst act of racist violence against the Little family—far from it. During Malcolm's childhood, his house would be burned to the ground and his father would die— likely murdered. Both were acts of retaliation against Earl Little, who had dared to challenge the status quo.

Earl Little grew up on a farm in Reynolds, Georgia, during the heart of the Jim Crow era. *Jim Crow* meant segregation in the South. Although black Americans had become first-class citizens under federal law after the Civil War, local and state legislatures in the South created laws that imposed segregation—technically, this meant "separate" and almost always meant "inferior." Schools, streetcars, restaurants, restrooms, drinking fountains, pools, beaches, movie houses, churches, and many more facilities in the South were segregated.

In addition, blacks in the South could not vote without fear of retribution, meaning harassment, bodily harm, or being fired from their job. By dominating the vote, whites

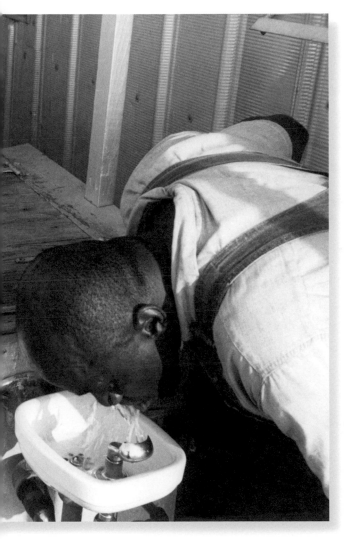

During the Jim Crow era, black and white Americans were not allowed to drink from the same water fountains.

completely dominated political offices and thus were able to perpetuate segregation. Blacks were essentially barred from good-paying jobs, virtually banned from nice neighborhoods, and prevented from dating white people (an act that was often punished by death). Blacks were expected to refer to whites reverentially ("yes, sir") while being referred to as "boy," "coon," and "nigger." If a black person broke a law—or in Earl Little's case, challenged the white caste system—punishment was exceptionally harsh.

Typical of black Southerners, Little dropped out of school around the third or fourth grade. But he was a smart man who craved independence. Little took the bold step of moving to Canada, settling in the French-speaking city of Montreal. In 1919, he married Louise Norton from Grenada, a British island in the Caribbean.

Louise and Earl Little

Louise was a biracial beauty: tall and thin with long, flowing hair. Her mother had died when she was a child, and all she knew about her father was that he was a white man with red hair. At the time, it was not unusual for white men to have sex (often forcibly) with black women and then take no responsibility. The resulting children grew up fatherless and usually poor, with the stigma of being racial "mongrels," as southern racists called them. Louise at least received more education than most black and biracial children.

In the 1920s, Earl and Louise followed the teachings of Marcus Garvey, head of the Universal Negro Improvement Association (UNIA). Garvey preached that there was no future for blacks in America.

"For the Negro to depend on the ballot and his industrial progress alone, will be hopeless," he wrote, "as it does not help him when he is lynched, burned, jim crowed and segregated."

For Garvey, there was only one solution. American blacks should return to Africa, where they would help Africans create an advanced and independent society.

While this goal seemed lofty and, indeed, far-fetched, Garvey inspired feelings of self-pride and independence among his followers, including Earl and Louise. A carpenter

Marcus Garvey

by trade, Earl also preached the teachings of the UNIA. Louise helped the organization as a writer and bookkeeper. The couple was tempting its fate, since white supremacists often retaliated against UNIA members—especially vocal leaders, like Earl. Those in the North were not spared. In the 1920s, the Ku Klux Klan reached its greatest heights, with some 4 million members nationwide.

The Littles moved often and had lots of children. Wilfred was born in Philadelphia, and Hilda and Philbert were born in Omaha, Nebraska. On May 19, 1925—not many weeks after Klansmen had shattered the Littles' windows—Louise gave birth to Malcolm Little (no middle name). For young Malcolm, it would be a turbulent childhood.

Threatened by whites for his preachings (he was president of the UNIA's Omaha branch), Earl moved the family out of Nebraska. They lived in Milwaukee, Wisconsin, and then Albion, Michigan, before buying a farmhouse on the outskirts of Lansing, Michigan. But whites in the area, who did not want a black family in the neighborhood, sued to have the sale of the house reversed. A clause in the deed, they pointed out, stated that the land should never be occupied "by persons other than those of the Caucasian race."

Earl vowed to keep his home but to no avail. In late November 1929, in the middle of the night, whites set fire to the Little house. Amid the smoke and roaring flames, Earl and Louise managed to get their five children (including a baby) out of the house. The fire department arrived but did not attempt to put out the flames. As the Little family shivered in the cold, their home and all their belongings burned to the ground.

The Littles moved to a house in East Lansing, where white neighbors welcomed them by stoning their house. Unwanted anywhere, it seemed, Earl built his own house in a rural area in the outskirts of Lansing. Finally, it appeared, they found some peace.

With several acres of land, the family grew vegetables and raised chickens and rabbits. Louise would have eight children in all; after Malcolm came Reginald, Yvonne, and Wesley. Louise ran the household, cooking, cleaning, and making sure the older children did their homework. She strongly believed in the power of education.

Within the home, however, tensions brewed. Louise and Earl often argued, and Earl sometimes hit his wife. Malcolm often fought with his siblings, and he frequently screamed to get what he wanted. He recalled the story of buttered biscuits. When his siblings asked their mother for one, she would say no and they would acquiesce. But Malcolm would cry out and fuss until she gave in.

"So early in life," he wrote, "I had learned that if you want something, you had better make some noise."

Malcolm enjoyed the several acres of property that the family owned, and he even grew vegetables on his own little plot of land. He was proud when his mother served the peas he had grown for dinner. In the summertime, he enjoyed lying in the garden and staring up at the floating clouds, thinking about all kinds of things.

While Malcolm attended church with his family, he never embraced religion. He was, however, inspired by his father's rousing speeches. Malcolm often traveled with his father to UNIA meetings, held in people's living rooms.

> "I remember," Malcolm wrote, "how the meetings always closed with my father saying, several times, and the people chanting up after him, 'Up, you mighty race, you can accomplish what you will!'"

But the Black Legion, a Ku Klux Klan splinter group, was on to Malcolm's father, and they started to threaten him again. In late September 1931, he needed to leave town on an errand, but Louise pleaded with him to stay. Earl didn't listen—and he didn't come back.

On September 28, 1931, the children were awakened by their mother's screams. Police had arrived with the news: Earl Little was dead.

The headlines of a local paper reported the incident: "Man Run Over by Street Car; Believe Negro Lost Life Because He Forgot Coat . . . ." But Louise did not believe it was an accident. She insisted that he had been murdered by those who had been threatening him. The police stated that Earl had been alive when they came to his aid and that he had said that he had slipped and fallen in front of the streetcar.

Malcolm insisted that was a lie: "My father's skull, on one side, was crushed in, I was told later. Negroes in Lansing have always whispered that he was attacked, and then laid across some tracks for a streetcar to run over him. His body was cut almost in half."

Louise was hysterical at the funeral, and upsetting news followed shortly thereafter. Earl had taken out two insurance policies, a small one and a larger one. Louise received payment on the first one, just a few hundred dollars, but the insurance company refused to pay on the second one, claiming they didn't have to because it was a suicide. Such a claim seemed preposterous. As Malcolm put it, "how could my father bash himself in the head, then get down across the streetcar tracks to be run over?"

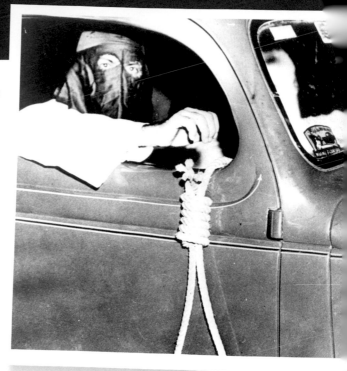

Louise, thirty-four years old, now faced an impossible challenge: providing for eight kids in the heart of the Great Depression.

Masked Ku Klux Klansman

Wilfred, the eldest child, helped by quitting school and working odd jobs. Hilda also stepped up by caring for the babies. Because of her light complexion, Louise frequently found work in Lansing as a maid and seamstress for whites. But according to Malcolm, she would always be fired once they found out that she was a Negro. She would come home crying, frightened for her family's future.

As much as it hurt Louise's pride, the Littles went on welfare. They received a small check and free food, but it wasn't nearly enough. The children would walk two miles to Lansing, where they'd buy day-old bread and cookies for a nickel. If they were lucky, they'd have stewed tomatoes with bread for dinner. At worst, it was a bowl of dandelion greens. Desperate for food and money, Malcolm and his brothers shot rabbits, trapped muskrats, and speared bullfrogs, selling the frog meat to a white family. Sometimes dizzy from hunger, Malcolm walked to Lansing and stole apples and other food.

He also hung out at the Gohannases, who let him stay for supper. Mr. and Mrs. Gohannas were a nice older couple who raised their nephew "Big Boy," a friend of Malcolm.

As if Louise didn't have enough worries, welfare workers began to meddle in the family's affairs, which angered her to no end. The workers believed that some of the children should be sent to foster homes, and they planted seeds of dissension. They criticized Louise for turning down free pork, unconcerned that eating pork was against her religion (Seventh Day Adventist). They asked the children disturbing questions, such as who was the smartest one and why did Malcolm look different than the others.

Malcolm had lighter skin and reddish-brown hair, traits inherited from his white maternal grandfather. During the Jim Crow era, light-skinned blacks actually held a higher status in their culture. Some black Americans bought lightening cream for their skin, and others held exclusive "paper bag parties," inviting only those Negroes whose skin was lighter than a paper bag. But Malcolm was often teased about his unusual look. He later grew to hate his "whiteness," for it reminded him of the red-haired man whom he felt had raped his grandmother.

Race was a constant factor in Malcolm's life. A photograph of his fourth-grade class at Pleasant Grove Elementary School shows thirty-two white children and Malcolm, who towers over his classmates. While southern schools were segregated (by state law) and many northern schools were segregated (by custom), Pleasant Grove accepted the Little kids. There were not enough black children in the community to establish an all-black school, and a handful of black students in one school were not considered a "threat."

Inside a dilapidated school for black children in Georgia, 1941

An exceptionally smart child, Malcolm brought home good grades. He fought with white kids on occasion, but he played with them too. They often called the Little kids "darkie" and "nigger," but all thought it was just harmless teasing. None of the children understood the deep-rooted racism behind those loaded words.

Though school was not particularly troublesome for Malcolm, his family life began to deteriorate. Welfare workers continued to put pressure on Louise to send her kids to foster homes, so much so that she showed signs of mentally "cracking." Her spirits and hopes lifted when it appeared that a man whom she was dating would marry her or at least support the family. But he jilted her in 1936 or '37, and afterward she was never the same. Louise began talking to herself and seemed unaware of others in the room.

The fatherless Little children were gradually losing their mother, who became less responsible and less responsive. "We children watched our anchor giving way," Malcolm later wrote. "It was something terrible that you couldn't get your hands on, yet you couldn't get away from. It was a sensing that something bad was going to happen."

Louise's mental breakdown was the last straw for the welfare workers, who began sending the children to live with other families. Malcolm was sent to live with the Gohannases, where he shared a room with his friend Big Boy. Malcolm was torn between missing his family and enjoying the normalcy of his new home. He and Big Boy, both of whom attended West Junior High School in Lansing, often fished and hunted together.

Whenever Malcolm returned home to visit his family, he found his mother sinking deeper into mental illness. It wasn't long before she was committed to the state mental hospital in Kalamazoo, an hour and a half away. Over the years, Malcolm would occasionally visit her at the hospital, but her condition degenerated to the point where she didn't even recognize him. He would stop visiting her in 1952, and the family took her out of the hospital in 1963.

To his dying days, Malcolm blamed the welfare workers for driving his mother insane. "I truly believe that if ever a state social agency destroyed a family, it destroyed ours," he wrote. "We wanted and tried to stay together. Our home didn't have to be destroyed. But the Welfare, the courts, and their doctor, gave us the one-two-three punch. And ours was not the only case of this kind."

With their mother committed, the children became wards of the state, and their fate was determined by a judge named McClellan. Malcolm stayed with the Gohannases, while

Wilfred and Hilda were allowed to stay in the family home. The other five children were divided up among three different families. The children tried their best to stay in touch with each other. Though separated by distance, they were still a close family.

Removed from his family home, Malcolm drifted into the sea of life, beginning an aimless but highly eventful adventure.

Following in the footsteps of his brother Philbert, Malcolm tried to make it as an amateur boxer. Participants had to be sixteen years old, which Malcolm claimed he was even though he was just thirteen. Too young and too inexperienced, Malcolm retired at 0-2, losing decisively both times to a white kid named Bill Peterson. (In the second bout, he was kayoed at the opening bell!)

An exterior view of the state mental hospital in Kalamazoo

Malcolm "Red" Little

After getting knocked out in the ring, Malcolm got kicked out of junior high because of a series of mischievous deeds, culminated by the placing of a tack on his teacher's chair. A state official, Maynard Allen, removed Malcolm from the Gohannases and sent him to live in a detention home with the Swerlins, a white couple, in Mason, Michigan.

Mrs. Swerlin was a big woman with a robust laugh, while her husband was thin with a black mustache. Both were exceptionally nice to the kids in the detention home, even letting the less-serious offenders, including Malcolm, eat with them at dinner. Malcolm was troubled by how casually they used the word *nigger*, but otherwise he was happy in the home. The Swerlins liked him, too. Though Malcolm was supposed to be sent to reform school, the couple arranged to have him go to Mason Junior High, where he would join the Lyons children as the only black kids in the school.

Malcolm found the white students to be exceptionally friendly, and he quickly fit in. He joined the debate society and the basketball team, and he excelled academically. In the second semester of seventh grade, he even was elected class president. While Malcolm initially enjoyed the attention, he gradually realized that he wasn't "fitting in" at all. He began to feel like a novelty, a mascot—someone who whites may have liked but would never accept fully into their lives. As Malcolm put it, "I was unique in my class, like a pink poodle."

Malcolm recalled his history teacher making nigger jokes and laughing about African Americans' supposed lack of contributions to history. Malcolm attended school dances, but he knew there was no way he could dance with a white girl. When he traveled with his school basketball team, opposing fans showered him with racial epithets.

While all the African Americans that Malcolm knew were at least somewhat ashamed of being black, he finally met someone who wasn't: his half-sister Ella, a young woman from his father's first marriage. Big, dark-skinned, and successful, Ella lived with family members in Boston. When she came to visit her half-siblings, Malcolm immediately liked her. She was self-confident with a loving nature, and she praised a proud Malcolm when he showed her his sterling report card.

In the summer of 1940, Malcolm visited Ella and his two other half-siblings in Roxbury, the black section of Boston. Malcolm had never been in an all-black community before, and he was enamored by what he saw. Restaurants, nightclubs, pool halls, and, on Sundays, churches, were filled with African Americans. By the looks of the cars they drove, Malcolm knew they were successful. Ella's previous husband was a doctor, and her second husband was a soldier. Her brother Earl was a successful singer and showman.

When Malcolm returned to Mason for eighth grade, he was not the same person. He felt like a fish out of water—that he should be with his people in Boston and not stuck as a "mascot" in Mason. Although he continued to excel in the classroom, he was no longer the happy-go-lucky Malcolm. One particular incident took him over the edge. Mr. Ostrowski, an English teacher whom Malcolm liked and respected, asked him what he'd like to be when he grew up. Malcolm wasn't sure, but he said he might want to be a lawyer. He remembered the teacher's response:

"Mr. Ostrowski looked surprised, I remember, and leaned back in his chair and clasped his hands behind his head. He kind of half-smiled and said, 'Malcolm, one of life's first needs is for us to be realistic. Don't misunderstand me, now. We all here like you, you know that. But you've got to be realistic about being a nigger. A lawyer—that's no realistic goal for a nigger. You need to think about something you *can* be. You're good with your hands—making things. Everybody admires your carpentry shop work. Why don't you plan on carpentry? People like you as a person—you'd get all kinds of work.'"

The teacher's words hit harder than Bill Peterson's punches. Mr. Ostrowski encouraged the white students to pursue their preferred professions, and they were worse students than Malcolm. He began to shut down. From then on, he hated sitting through Mr. Ostrowski's class. When someone said the word *nigger*, he gave them a hard look. Mrs. Swerlin and others kept asking him what was wrong, and he always said nothing. It reached a point where the Swerlins and Mr. Allen agreed to send him to the home of the Lyones, the black family in town. With Mrs. Swerlin fighting back tears, Malcolm said goodbye.

Malcolm lived with the Lyones for two months, until he finished eighth grade, but he knew that Mason held no future for him. Every other day, he wrote to Ella, and he asked her if he could live with her. She said yes, and just days after he graduated, Malcolm boarded a Greyhound bus for Boston.

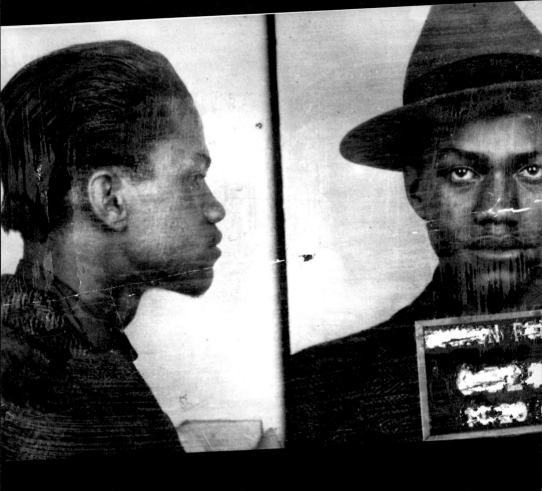

Police mug shot of Malcolm at age twenty-five

3

INCARCERATION
AND SALVATION

WHEN MALCOLM ARRIVED in the Roxbury section
of Boston, he quickly noticed class differences—within
the black race. Blacks on "the Hill," including Ella,
considered themselves more cultured and dignified than
those in the "ghetto." A Hill man might work as a janitor
in a bank, but his friends would say he worked in the
banking profession. Ella wanted Malcolm to immerse
himself in this refined black culture, and she hoped he
would fulfill her dream for him by becoming a lawyer.

But Malcolm disliked the pretentiousness of the Hill
crowd; instead, he felt at home in the ghetto. "That world
of grocery stores, walk-up flats, cheap restaurants, poolrooms,
bars, storefront churches, and pawnshops seemed to hold a
natural lure for me," he wrote.

Malcolm stared through the window of a poolroom
so much that one of the workers finally came out to say
hello. He was a friendly, slick-haired "cat" named Shorty
who also happened to be from Lansing. Calling Malcolm
his "homeboy," Shorty took him under his wing. He would
introduce him to the sordid side of Roxbury, a world of jazz,

gambling, interracial dating, drugs, and hustling. It wasn't long before Shorty found Malcolm a job as a shoeshine boy at the Roseland State Ballroom—much to Ella's dismay. The man he was replacing, Freddie, had just quit after "hitting the numbers" (the equivalent of winning the lottery, although it was illegal at the time). Freddie bought himself a Cadillac and trained Malcolm as his replacement.

All the great swing bands of the 1940s played at the Roseland, entertaining whites on some nights and black audiences on others. On Malcolm's first day at the ballroom, the world-famous Benny Goodman band was preparing to play. Freddie taught his protégé how to shine shoes with flair and, whenever he got the chance, head to the men's room to hand out towels. To make the best tips possible, Freddie said, Malcolm should "Uncle Tom" a little—butter up the white folks.

A man dressed in a zoot suit
dances the night away with his partner.

Malcolm fully immersed himself in this lifestyle by purchasing a zoot suit (long, loose jacket with high-waist, baggy trousers) and conking his hair, like Shorty's. Conking involved a mixture of raw eggs and a harsh chemical called lye, which caused a horrific burning sensation when rubbed onto the scalp. But the result was straight, slick-backed hair, which was considered sharp in the inner cities of the day.

Ella, determined to get Malcolm on the right path, got him a job at Townsend Drug and Soda Fountain in her neighborhood. But when his shift was over, he would head back down to the ghetto, where he partied all night. When the United States entered World War II in December 1941, and hundreds of thousands of American men enlisted in the service, better job opportunities opened up for teenagers. Ella got Malcolm a job working for the New Haven Railroad. He toiled as a sandwich boy and dishwasher on the *Yankee Clipper*, a train that ran from Boston to New York. Ella was glad to remove Malcolm from the sins of Roxbury; unfortunately, it introduced him to the nightlife of Harlem, the vibrant black section of New York. Malcolm was mesmerized.

During his layovers in New York, he hung out at such high-class nightspots as Small's Paradise and the Braddock Hotel. He became such a regular that bartenders poured "Red" (his new nickname, based on his hair color) his favorite drink whenever he walked in. Malcolm hung out with musicians, danced with the ladies, and spent his earnings on liquor and reefer (marijuana). He was often inebriated when he returned to the train, and after several complaints about his behavior, he was told to find another job. He got one—as a waiter at Small's Paradise.

A U.S. Army soldier dances at the racially mixed Savoy Ballroom in Harlem, New York City, in February 1942.

In 1943, Malcolm turned eighteen. That meant he was eligible to be drafted into the military. During the war, most American men felt it was their duty to serve their country. Not Malcolm. His goal was to arrive at the induction center acting crazy. Donning a zoot suit with yellow shoes and frizzled-up hair, he ran his mouth nonstop. After telling a military psychiatrist that he wanted to organize southern black soldiers and kill some "crackers," he was labeled 4-F—unfit for military service.

For the duration of the war, 1943 to 1945, Malcolm engaged in his most destructive behavior, constantly flirting with danger. He dated a blonde woman, whom he called Sophia. He had met her at the Roseland in Boston, and they continued to see each other in New York. Throughout most of the country, interracial dating was taboo—in fact, it could get a black man killed in the South. But in the upscale, interracial ballrooms of Roxbury and Harlem, race mixing was not unheard of. While Ella frowned upon his relationship with Sophia, Malcolm's friends admired him. Among his crowd, a black man had really scored big if he was dating a white woman. Even after Sophia married a well-to-do white man in Boston, she continued to date and party with Malcolm.

By this time, Malcolm became known by his friends as "Detroit Red." They associated Michigan, his home state, with Detroit. While jumping from job to job, Malcolm also hustled on the streets. He carried a gun, committed robberies, and got high on cocaine to summon the courage for those crimes. To feed his cocaine addiction, he stole more often. Also around this time, Malcolm allegedly began having sex with men for money.

At one point in 1945, several men wanted to kill Detroit Red. They included bar owners who mistakenly thought Malcolm had robbed them, a fellow crook whom Malcolm had punched, and his friend West Indian Archie, who felt Malcolm had tried to cheat him in the numbers game. At the urging of Malcolm's friend Sammy, Shorty drove to New York and took Malcolm back home.

When Malcolm returned to Boston:

"Ella couldn't believe how atheist, how uncouth I had become," Malcolm later wrote. "Every word I spoke was hip or profane. I would bet that my working vocabulary wasn't two hundred words."

After moving in with Shorty, Malcolm spent most of his time sleeping, smoking cigarettes (up to four packs a day), and getting high—mostly on marijuana but sometimes on cocaine. Sophia, still married, continued to see him, supplying him with more and more money for his drug habit even though he physically abused her.

Sophia seemed to do whatever Malcolm asked her to, and her younger sister—who at this time was dating Shorty—did what Sophia told her to do. So when Malcolm and Shorty (along with their friend Rudy) asked them to help them burglarize houses, they agreed. Working in a wealthy white neighborhood, the five of them robbed house after house. The sisters would enter the houses, posing as saleswomen or pollsters. They scoped out the homes and then provided the details to the three men, who would use those clues to break into and rob the homes.

The group knocked off numerous houses until police began to hone in on Malcolm as a suspect. When he took in a stolen watch for repairs, while carrying a concealed gun, he was arrested. Back at Malcolm's apartment, police found their stolen loot, including furs and jewelry. Malcolm knew he was going to prison. In fact, he received a maximum sentence for burglary: eight to ten years. Since he had only one prior arrest, on a minor charge, Malcolm thought he should have received a lighter sentence—and that he would have if he weren't black and if he hadn't induced white women to join his operation (and had an affair with one of them).

That may have been true, yet Malcolm Little had engaged in criminal activity repeatedly. Years later, he would fully recognize "how bad, how evil, I was."

In February 1946, Malcolm was transported to Charlestown State Prison, a rat-infested hellhole that dated back to 1805. His cell was so small that he could touch both walls at the same time. Each prisoner was given a bucket in which to urinate and defecate, creating a nauseating stench throughout the row of cells. Without drugs, Malcolm was a physical wreck and extremely agitated. He cursed out the prison psychologist and chaplain as well as God and the Bible. He was so wicked, the prisoners called him "Satan."

Charlestown State Prison

Malcolm had sunk so low in life that there was nowhere to go but up. Meeting Bimbi, a fellow prisoner, was his first step up the ladder.

Malcolm met Bimbi while working in the license plate shop. A red-haired African American like Malcolm, Bimbi was a longtime prisoner who had spent his lonely hours reading about history, philosophy, and other subjects. When he talked, others listened. Malcolm respected Bimbi immensely, so when he told Malcolm that he was a smart guy and that he should take advantage of the prison's correspondence courses, Malcolm took his advice. He took a class in English—his first class of any kind since junior high school—and improved his grammar to the point where he could write a decent letter. Later, he would take a course in Latin.

Jackie Robinson

In early 1947, Malcolm was transferred to Concord Reformatory in Concord, Massachusetts. That spring, he became a huge fan of Jackie Robinson, the Brooklyn Dodgers second baseman who broke Major League Baseball's color barrier on April 15. Malcolm listened to Dodgers games on the radio, and he was so enamored with this black pioneer that he recalculated his batting average after every one of his at-bats. What Malcolm could not calculate were the odds of him joining Robinson as one of the great figures in black history. At the time, the odds of such a scenario were infinitesimal.

While in prison, Malcolm received letters from his siblings, five of whom had joined a burgeoning religious organization called the Nation of Islam. Philbert urged Malcolm to join, but Malcolm responded with a rude letter. However, a letter from Reginald in 1948 intrigued him. "Malcolm," he wrote, "don't eat any more pork, and don't smoke any more cigarettes. I'll show you how to get out of prison."

Get out of prison? Malcolm speculated that Reginald knew some clever scheme—like how acting crazy had kept him out of the military. Malcolm finished his pack of cigarettes and never smoked another one in his life. When pork was served a few days later, he passed. Malcolm did not hear from Reginald, but he was nonetheless proud of his self-discipline.

Norfolk State Prison

In late 1948, he got a tremendous break when the ever-resourceful Ella got him transferred to Norfolk Prison Colony. An experimental prison, its purpose was to rehabilitate criminals. Norfolk had flushing toilets, and each prisoner had his own room—with no bars. Instructors from universities, including Harvard, came to talk, and inmates engaged in group discussions and debates. Over his remaining years in prison, Malcolm would take full advantage of Norfolk's impressive library, reading voraciously.

But what about Reginald's message? Malcolm's younger brother finally came to see him. After a good deal of small talk, Reginald got down to it. God is a man, he said, and his name is Allah. He added that the devil is also a man. "What do you mean?" Malcolm asked. Reginald tipped his head toward some white inmates. "Them," he said. "The white man is the devil. . . . Without any exception."

White people, then and now, would resent such a statement, and most people consider the accusation preposterous. But to the Little family, including Malcolm, it seemed to make sense. Struck by his brother's words, Malcolm looked back on all the white people he had known: the racist men who had smashed his home's windows, burned his house down, and likely killed his father; the social workers who had broken up his family and helped drive his mother insane; the small-town folks who had called him "darkie" and "nigger"; Mr. Ostrowski, the dream-killing English teacher; the judge who had slapped him with the maximum sentence; and many others. The white man is the devil—it made perfect sense to Malcolm.

Reginald revisited Malcolm a few days later and explained that whites had stripped black Americans of their identity when they brought them to America as slaves. "You don't even know your true family name," Reginald said, "you wouldn't recognize your true language if you heard it." *Little* was the name of a white slave owner. Even religion, Reginald said, had been imposed on black people: Slaves had adopted Christianity from their slave owners.

Malcolm began to receive letters every day from family members who had joined the Nation of Islam. All of them urged him to join the Nation. They wrote that Islam was the black people's true religion. NOI leader Elijah Muhammad, a small and gentle man, was a messenger from Allah, they said. In Detroit, Muhammad had met Wallace D. Fard, the founder of the Nation of Islam whom Muhammad claimed was God personified.

Muhammad preached that his members should live clean lives, praise Allah, love each other, and respect themselves and others. By abstaining from pork and cigarettes, as well as liquor and other vices, Malcolm would be closer to Allah and released from his spiritual prison.

Elijah Muhammad

The one thing that made NOI different from other religions (and would catch the attention of the FBI) was that it was racially exclusive. Members believed in independence and self-sufficiency for blacks, not integration. They believed that blacks could never live in harmony with whites, because the latter had been and were still oppressors.

Muhammad told the story of Yakub, a big-headed scientist who had lived 6,000 years ago. According to this elaborate fable, the original people on earth were black but Yakub created a white race, which was savage and evil. Eventually, whites rose to power and dominated the world, oppressing all other races. When Malcolm's sister Hilda relayed this story to Malcolm, he was left speechless.

Malcolm not only wanted to join the Nation of Islam, he wrote a letter to Elijah Muhammad, redoing it numerous times to get it right. He was thrilled when Muhammad responded. He recalled:

"It had an all but electrical effect upon me to see the signature of the 'Messenger of Allah.' After he welcomed me into the 'true knowledge,' he gave me something to think about. The black prisoner, he said, symbolized white society's crime of keeping black men oppressed and deprived and ignorant, and unable to get decent jobs, turning them into criminals. He told me to have courage. He even enclosed some money for me, a five-dollar bill."

Over his remaining years in prison, Malcolm would become something of a hermit. He wrote daily letters to Muhammad and to any former friend he could think of, spreading the word of Allah and the Nation of Islam. He was so anxious to read, write, and educate himself that he transcribed the entire dictionary. Malcolm read with fascination about the history of Africa and other civilizations. He learned all the sordid details of the slave trade, when Europeans and Americans captured Africans and brought them in chains to their countries, where they were stripped of their freedom, family, identity, and dignity.

Malcolm wasn't interested in whitewashed American history books. Instead, he paged through *Story of Civilization* by Will Durant, *Souls of Black Folk* by W. E. B. Du Bois, and *Negro History* by Carter G. Woodson. He learned about black heroes and rebels, including a man named Nat Turner who had led a great slave uprising. Malcolm read about Egypt, Ethiopia, and China as well as the works of German philosophers Arthur Schopenhauer, Immanuel Kant, and Friedrich Nietzsche. Reading up to fifteen hours a day, Malcolm gained a wide-ranging knowledge of the world and its history.

At Norfolk, Malcolm joined the debating program, which he fully enjoyed. To Malcolm, addressing an audience—sharing his knowledge, expounding his views, and spreading the word of Allah whenever he could—was exhilarating. He prepared thoroughly for each debate, anticipating his opponents' rebuttals and thinking up proper responses. These debating skills would come in handy years later, when white reporters would pepper him with questions.

In 1950, Malcolm was transferred back to Charlestown. He felt he was being punished for telling Norfolk inmates to join the Nation of Islam, which by that time was under FBI investigation. In Charlestown, however, Malcolm continued to spread the message. After being denied parole in 1951, Malcolm applied again in the summer of 1952. This time, parole was granted.

On August 7, 1952, after six and a half years of incarceration, Malcolm was a freed man—in more ways than one. He now looked forward to meeting the person who had changed his life, Elijah Muhammad.

4 EMPOWERING THE NOI

UPON HIS RELEASE from Charlestown, Malcolm's first stop was a Turkish bathhouse, where he literally and figuratively washed away the stench of prison. Hilda gave him some money, which he spent on three things: better eyeglasses, a wristwatch, and a suitcase. Prior to prison, Malcolm might have spent that money on cigarettes, liquor, and drugs, but he was entirely transformed. His new tools would help him with his new pursuits: reading, keeping appointments, and traveling to spread the word of Islam.

The traveling would come later. Initially, Malcolm settled in Detroit, where he lived and worked with his brother Wilfred. Malcolm found comfort in Wilfred's family routine. Devout Muslims, Wilfred and his wife and children cleansed themselves each morning before joining each other on the prayer rug. They would greet each other by softly saying, *"As-Salaam-Alaikum"* (Arabic for "Peace be unto you"), and they would reply with *"Wa-Alaikum-Salaam"* ("And unto you be peace"). After a breakfast of just juice and coffee, Wilfred and Malcolm went to work at a furniture store in a black section of Detroit.

Malcolm was disgusted with the white owners of the store, claiming that they sold cheap merchandise at inflated prices. They would offer the furniture on credit but with high interest rates that they hid in the fine print. For Malcolm, it was just another instance of the white man exploiting his people.

Malcolm found solace in the confines of Temple One, the home of the Nation of Islam's Detroit chapter. It was the first Nation of Islam temple, established by NOI founder Wallace Fard in 1931. At their Sunday services and weeknight meetings, members greeted each other in a dignified manner. Women wore full-length gowns and scarves that covered their heads, while men were dressed in conservative suits. The children impressed Malcolm with their proper manners.

Wallace Fard Muhammad in 1933

On the blackboard, someone had painted the American flag and Muslim flag. Under the former were the words "Slavery, Suffering and Death"; under the latter: "Islam: Freedom, Justice, Equality." To Malcolm, that just about said it all.

The only thing that bothered Malcolm was all the empty seats. Outside, dope dealers, hustlers, and prostitutes roamed

The University of Islam, adjacent to Temple Two in Chicago

the neighborhood. Why, Malcolm wondered, weren't these lost souls brought into the fold? He felt that the NOI was much too passive, that its members should go to the streets to recruit black citizens. Everyone needed to know the truth, he felt, and be saved like he had been.

Wilfred advised him to be patient, and soon Malcolm changed his focus. On Labor Day weekend, 1952, the Muslims of Detroit Temple Number One embarked on a road trip to Chicago to meet Elijah Muhammad. Malcolm was thrilled to meet the man he had idolized for all those years in prison. Combined, the Muslims of Temples One and Two (Chicago's chapter) numbered only a couple hundred, but for Malcolm it was a grand event. Muhammad was a little man, but he appeared majestic in his gold-embroidered fez while surrounded by the NOI's Fruit of Islam bodyguards.

At the conclusion of his address to the faithful, Muhammad called out Malcolm by name. He praised Malcolm for staying strong while in prison, and he expressed faith that he would continue to lead the good life.

Paradise Valley, a neighborhood in Detroit where many black businesses were located in the 1940s

Afterward, Muhammad invited his visitors to his home. Though in awe of his host, Malcolm engaged him in conversation. He asked how they could increase the membership in the Detroit chapter, and Muhammad responded that he should recruit the young people of the area. That was all Malcolm needed to hear. From that point on, he would become the greatest recruiter the organization had ever seen.

After work every day, Malcolm visited Detroit's poolrooms, bars, and street corners, not to partake in vice—like he had in the past—but to convince black Americans to attend a meeting at Temple One. Most everyone shrugged him off, but Malcolm was so persistent in this daily ritual that within a few months Temple One's membership had tripled. Malcolm's recruiting accomplishments were duly noted by the Honorable Elijah Muhammad.

Around this time, Malcolm changed his name from Little to X, a surname taken by many in the Nation of Islam. These members no longer wanted to be known by their slave name.

X stands for the unknown, making it a logical name for those slave descendants whose real names had been taken from them. If another Malcolm had joined the Detroit temple and wanted to change his name, he would be called Malcolm 2X. Subsequent Malcolms would have been Malcolm 3X, Malcolm 4X, etc.

In early 1953, Malcolm got a job doing cleanup work at a company that made garbage trucks. Of course, his true vocation was with the NOI, for whom he was appointed assistant minister of Temple One. Malcolm became a regular speaker at Temple One meetings. He loved to educate his followers about black history, often focusing on the horrors and injustice of slavery. Tall, commanding, and passionate, Malcolm spoke clearly and forcefully, capturing the full attention of everyone in the room.

He also captured the attention of the FBI. Anti-Communist fervor percolated throughout the 1950s, and the FBI agents investigated numerous organizations that they felt were anti-American, including the Nation of Islam. With the U.S. at war in Korea, FBI agents visited Malcolm and told him to register for the draft. When he arrived at the draft board, he declared himself exempt from the draft as a conscientious objector— one who refuses to be inducted because he or she believes that war violates his or her religious principles.

"They asked if I knew what 'conscientious objector' meant," Malcolm recalled. "I told them that when the white man asked me to go off somewhere and fight and maybe die to preserve the way the white man treated the black man in America, then my conscience made me object."

Louis X

Malcolm underwent a physical exam and was told his case would be "pending." He wouldn't hear from the board until 1960, when he was classified as "Class 5-A," over the age of military obligation (thirty-five). Later in the 1960s, Nation of Islam member Muhammad Ali—the legendary boxer and a friend of Malcolm—would declare himself a conscientious objector. He would be sentenced to five years in prison for dodging the draft (although he was able to avoid serving time).

While still living in Detroit, Malcolm got a job as an assembly line worker with Ford Motor Company. However, Elijah Muhammad had bigger plans for his talented recruiter. In 1954, he sent Malcolm X to Boston to help him expand Temple Eleven, a group so small that their meetings were held in a member's living room.

Malcolm's recruiting efforts were so good that the Boston branch expanded to a storefront location. His half-sister Ella (who would convert to Islam a few years later) beamed with pride, excited that Malcolm had turned his life around so dramatically. Notably, Louis X (formerly Louis Walcott, a singer nicknamed "The Charmer") became Malcolm's assistant minister in the Boston temple. Louis X would change his last name to Farrakhan, and in 1978 he would become the head of the Nation of Islam. Like Malcolm, Farrakhan would be an outspoken and polarizing figure.

Malcolm left Louis X in charge of the Boston temple and moved on to Philadelphia, where his recruiting and oratory skills expanded the membership of that NOI temple. Elijah Muhammad then sent Malcolm to Harlem, where his most challenging mission lay ahead.

From his personal experience, Malcolm knew that vice was rampant on the Harlem streets. One of his first goals was to save Sammy, one of his old partners in crime, but he was too late. Sammy had been found dead in his home, with $25,000 in his pockets.

More progressive than other black areas of the country, Harlem was already home to black separatist groups and preachers, many of whom shouted their message on street corners. Malcolm and his small group of local NOI members made the rounds of these areas. They condemned the white man's oppression and handed out fliers, urging Harlemites to attend NOI meetings. They also hung out at black storefront churches, where they encouraged congregates to abandon the white man's religion for Islam.

Not everyone who attended the NOI meetings came back. While many liked the message, few could adhere to the strict rules laid out by the Nation of Islam. Members were not allowed to eat pork or unhealthy foods or use tobacco, alcohol, or narcotics. They could not gamble, attend movies or sporting events, dance, date, or have sex. Nor could they go on long vacations or sleep longer than necessary. Black men were also told to be respectful and courteous to the women in their lives.

While building NOI's membership in Harlem, Malcolm ventured to other cities, starting temples in Hartford, Connecticut; Springfield, Massachusetts; and several other areas. When the Nation provided him with a car, he put 30,000 miles on the odometer in just five months. In 1955, Malcolm even started a temple in the Deep South—in a funeral home in Atlanta, Georgia.

Later that year, Rosa Parks and Martin Luther King Jr. would help launch a bus boycott in Montgomery, Alabama, an event that sparked the civil rights movement. King called for a movement that was nonviolent, and he hoped that one day blacks and whites would "sit down together at the table of brotherhood." While King called for integration, the NOI insisted that blacks could never live freely and fully in a white man's world. "We are against segregation because it is unjust," Malcolm said, but he added that "we are against integration because [it is] a false solution to a real problem."

Malcolm used the 1954 *Brown v. Board of Education* decision as a case in point. Hailed as one of the most important U.S. Supreme Court decisions in history, the court ruled that segregated public schools were unconstitutional. The belief that white-controlled governments and school boards would now integrate their schools turned out to be a false hope. Southerners ignored and resisted the high court's rulings for many years. Similarly, blacks had been granted the right to vote in 1870, yet by 1960 only 6.7 percent of blacks in Mississippi were registered to vote due to the exclusionary

and intimidation practices of whites in that state. So while King called for love between the races, Malcolm preached an entirely different message.

Nettie Hunt sits with her daughter on the steps of the Supreme Court the day following the Court's historic decision in *Brown v. Board of Education*.

When he wasn't recruiting and speaking, Malcolm continued to educate himself. He refined his oratory skills by studying the great Roman speaker Cicero as well as the white evangelical Christian preacher Billy Graham. Malcolm also found time to write a column called "God's Angry Men" for the *Amsterdam News*, a black Harlem newspaper.

Malcolm was a serious man with a stern expression, but in 1956 he found a soft spot for NOI member Betty Shabazz. Betty was the antithesis of Malcolm's only previous girlfriend, "Sophia," the blonde party girl who had shared in Malcolm's vices. Betty, who was studying to be a nurse, was serious about her faith and career.

Betty recalled when she first saw Malcolm: "He was tall, he was thin, and the way he was galloping it looked as though he was going someplace much more important than the podium. . . . [H]e got to the podium—and I sat up straight."

Malcolm not only respected Betty but found her attractive as well. Sometimes he took followers to visit museums and libraries, and when he did he always invited Betty. She became known as the woman who could melt his serious expression into a boyish grin.

Elijah Muhammad met Betty in Chicago and told Malcolm she would make a good wife. Malcolm agreed, and he eventually proposed to her—over the phone. Betty responded with an excited "yes," and the couple wed on January 14, 1958, in Lansing. That same day, Betty received her nursing license.

A policeman uses an attack dog on a civil rights demonstrator in Alabama.

A few months earlier, Malcolm was noticed by the mainstream media for the first time, as he was front and center in a racial incident on the streets of Harlem. In the 1950s, and well beyond, animosity between predominantly white police forces and black citizens simmered in America's large cities. To blacks, white officers were seen as symbols of oppression or even literal oppressors. Whenever a police officer used excessive force on a black person, his or her neighbors would seethe with rage. Incidents of police brutality would spark numerous race riots in the 1960s, including one in Harlem in 1964.

In the '50s, black citizens were not yet emboldened to "rise up" to the point of rioting. But on April 26, 1957, the bold stance of Malcolm's Temple Seven nearly inspired Harlemites to take action into their own hands.

It all started when two white officers broke up a disturbance between a black man and a woman on 125th Street and Lenox Avenue. Johnson X Hinton and several other Temple Seven members refused to leave the scene when the police started beating the man. One of the NOI men told an officer, "You're not in Alabama—this is New York." The officers proceeded to arrest Hinton, and one of them hit him on the head multiple times until blood covered his face.

The officers took Hinton to their precinct house, figuring that was the end of the disturbance. But a short time later, some fifty Fruit of Islam members gathered in rank formation in front of the police station, with a number of curious onlookers behind them. As the minister of Temple Seven, Malcolm demanded to see Hinton. The police, wary of a potential riot, let him in. Finding Hinton bathed in blood and semiconscious, Malcolm demanded that he be sent to the hospital.

As an ambulance drove Hinton fifteen blocks to Harlem Hospital, the NOI members followed on foot, with a large number of black citizens joining them. By the time they reached the hospital, the crowd had grown to nearly 2,000, putting police on edge. When Malcolm was assured that Hinton was receiving proper care, he gave a hand gesture to his fellow Muslims. They promptly left the scene, and the onlookers followed suit.

A chief inspector was struck by how much influence Malcolm X had over his people. The inspector turned to James Hicks, a reporter for the *Amsterdam News*, and said: "This is too much power for one man to have." The inspector proceeded to request information on Malcolm's criminal background, and he soon was scrutinized by the New York Police Department's Bureau of Special Services and Investigation (BOSS).

The Nation of Islam took an assertive step to show that it would not put up with police brutality. The NOI filed three lawsuits, and an all-white jury awarded $70,000 to Johnson X Hinton. It was the largest damage award that the City of New York ever paid in a police brutality case.

Malcolm X had entered the public consciousness for the first time. Two years later, he would be thrust into the national spotlight.

Malcolm being interviewed by a swarm of reporters

5

THE
NATIONAL
STAGE

FROM 1968 TO 2008, when he retired at age ninety, Mike Wallace was a hard-hitting investigative journalist for the CBS news show *60 Minutes*. But long before then, in July 1959, he hosted a TV documentary that shocked America.

In *The Hate That Hate Produced*, Wallace and Louis Lomax (the first-ever black television journalist) introduced to the general public the Nation of Islam, which Wallace called the "most powerful of the black supremacist groups." The film showed Louis X calling the white man the greatest "liar," "robber," "drunkard," "trouble-maker," "deceiver," "peace-breaker," and "murderer" on earth. The film also showed a University of Islam school, run by the NOI, where, Wallace said, "Muslim children are taught to hate the white man."

Lomax interviewed Elijah Muhammad, who said that black people were divine and whites were devils. Lomax also talked to Malcolm X on camera. Asked if all white people were evil, Malcolm replied that white people *collectively* were evil. "[W]e don't have any historic example where we have found that they have, collectively, as a people, done good,"

Malcolm said. He said that black children were taught the same lessons as white children "minus the little Black Sambo story and things that were taught to you and me when we were coming up, to breed that inferiority complex in us."

Malcolm during a TV interview

Wallace indicated that the NOI was a hate-filled extremist group that was potentially dangerous to American society. At the end of the telecast, he asked for the support of black leaders who were "counseling patience and the relatively slow operation of legal measures."

The Hate That Hate Produced generated a tremendous amount of buzz, which had good and bad repercussions for the Nation of Islam. The telecast achieved Elijah Muhammad's goal of increasing membership, which doubled to some 60,000 within three weeks after it aired. But logistically, NOI leaders had a difficult time handling the great influx of new members.

Of greater concern was white backlash. Millions of whites watched or heard about the show and resented the accusations that they were white devils. For decades, the NOI had been "under the radar"; they had been able to call the white race "devils" without whites hearing the message. Now, white America was paying attention. The FBI responded by planting black informants in the Nation of Islam, and they paid particularly close attention to the words and actions of Malcolm X.

The documentary immediately thrust Malcolm into the national, even international, arena. Reporters from all over the country, and as far away as Paris and Stockholm, called

Malcolm, asking him why the Nation of Islam taught black supremacy and hate.

Every time he heard that question:

"something chemical happened inside me," he wrote. "When we Muslims had talked about 'the devil white man' he had been relatively abstract, someone we Muslims rarely actually came in contact with, but now here was that devil-in-the-flesh on the phone—with all of his calculating, cold-eyed, self-righteous tricks and nerve and gall. The voices questioning me became to me as breathing living devils."

Then as now, outsiders found it difficult to understand the NOI's message. In the above excerpt, Malcolm writes that *devil* was an abstract term, but then in the next sentence he personifies the term. In the documentary, Malcolm said that whites were evil not individually but collectively, which also caused a good deal of head-scratching. In his early years with the Nation, Malcolm's intention was to pass along the messages of Elijah Muhammad. But as the 1960s would progress, he would insert his own opinions more and more often, making it more difficult to discern between his views and the Nation's.

After the telecast, Roy Wilkins of the NAACP—the most prominent and the most conservative of the major civil

Roy Wilkins

rights organizations—strongly denounced the Nation of Islam. In discussing the NOI, Wilkins said that the "NAACP opposes and regards as dangerous any group, white or black, political or religious, that preaches hatred among men." Martin Luther King referred to the NOI as "one of the hate groups rising in our midst."

Thurgood Marshall, the legendary attorney who had won the landmark *Brown v. Board of Education* case on behalf of the NAACP, believed that the NOI's message could create white backlash and thus damage the efforts of the civil rights movement. In an address at Princeton University, Marshall derided the NOI as being "run by a bunch of thugs organized from prisons and jails." Malcolm had nothing good to say about Marshall, calling him a "twentieth century Uncle Tom."

Thurgood Marshall

While the Nation took a beating in many media circles, some black journalists were willing to see all sides of the organization. Wrote George S. Schuyler of the *Pittsburgh Courier*, a prominent black newspaper:

"Mr. Muhammad may be a rogue and a charlatan, but when anybody can get tens of thousands of Negroes to practice economic solidarity, respect their women, alter their atrocious diet, give up liquor, stop crime, juvenile deliquency and adultery, he is doing more for the Negro's welfare than any current leader I know."

Surely, the Nation deserved credit for transforming many of its members' lives. Rarely discussed is its unique, six-step strategy to help drug addicts. After the addicts admitted they had a problem (step one), they went through step two. In that stage, the addict was taught that segregation and racism made black Americans feel inferior, and that those with self-hatred and low self-esteem used drugs to help them escape their emotional pain.

In the late 1950s, Malcolm X entered a new phase of his extraordinary life. He and Betty became parents in November 1958 with the birth of their daughter Attallah. Their second child, a daughter named Qubilah, entered the world on Christmas Day, 1960. The couple would have four more daughters in later years: Ilyasah in 1962, Gamilah in 1964, and twins Malaak and Malikah in 1965.

Malcolm has been described as a loving father who liked to read poetry to his girls. Although trained as a nurse, Betty stayed home to raise her children and assist Malcolm. When she wasn't cooking, cleaning, and changing diapers, Betty answered Malcolm's many phone calls and typed and proofread his speeches. She was a dutiful wife.

Malcolm holding his daughter Ilyasah

Unfortunately for Betty and their daughters, Malcolm was frequently on the road. Besides his immense duties as a leader of the Nation of Islam, he became a national celebrity among blacks and liberals and was asked to speak on college campuses across the country.

A major reason for Malcolm's rise in popularity was the changing times. With the Great Depression and World War II well behind them, many Americans—particularly the millions who had become college educated after the war—were more progressive and open-minded. America was on the verge of a cultural revolution—one that would flourish in mid-decade. Even as early as 1960, the cultural zeitgeist (spirit of the times) was changing. When the young, progressive John F. Kennedy was inaugurated as president in January 1961 after years of the conservative Eisenhower administration, he announced that "the torch has been passed to a new generation of Americans."

The civil rights movement was changing as well. After the orderly Montgomery bus boycott in 1956, activists engaged in some smaller boycotts and protests, yet the movement was largely dormant until February 1, 1960. That day, four black college students (including one who would later convert to Islam) staged a sit-in in Greensboro, North Carolina, at a whites-only lunch counter, stating that they would not leave their stools until they were served. Their courageous action sparked a firestorm of sit-ins across the country. Feeling strength in numbers,

A group of North Carolina A & T students who were refused service in the second day of the Woolworth sit-in in 1960 thousands of young black Americans—often supported by white liberals—demanded justice immediately.

This grassroots movement was much different than the efforts of the NAACP, which largely sought justice through the legal system. Young black Americans—entrenched in poverty, unable to vote, and denied access to decent neighborhoods and jobs—did not want to sit around for years hoping that a law or two might be passed and that the white establishment might enforce such laws.

As sit-ins became increasingly successful (forcing more and more establishments to desegregate), young black Americans became emboldened. Many joined the Student Nonviolent Coordinating Committee (SNCC), which was formed during the sit-in craze and would help stage such legendary civil rights events as the Freedom Rides and Freedom Summer.

Progressive whites supported this assertive black movement, and southern segregationists opposed it. But those in the middle of the spectrum simply accepted it, which led to a permissive environment for outspoken activists to speak their minds—including Malcolm X.

While blacks and progressives followed Malcolm with increased curiosity, so did the FBI—especially in September 1960. That month, Cuban premier Fidel Castro flew to New York to address the United Nations. At the time, Castro was despised by the U.S. government. A year earlier, he had overthrown a corrupt Cuban government that had been friendly with the United States. After the U.S. refused to ally with him, he took over U.S.-owned property, businesses, and oil refineries in Cuba and entered a strong alliance with the Soviet Union. That fall, the U.S. began a covert campaign to oust Castro from power.

When visiting New York that September, Castro stayed at
Hotel Theresa in Harlem. Rarely had dignitaries chosen to
stay in this black section of New York, but many of Cuba's
citizens were black and Castro considered himself a champion
of the oppressed. He
had heard of Malcolm
X, the black man
who (like Castro) had
vocally opposed the
U.S. government, and
he requested a meeting
with him. The two met
behind closed doors
for nearly an hour.
Malcolm tried to recruit
Castro to the Nation of
Islam, and the Cuban
leader invited him to his country. As a courtesy gesture,
Malcolm offered Castro the use of the Fruit of Islam
bodyguards for his protection, if needed.

Fidel Castro with Malcolm at the
Hotel Theresa in Harlem

The meeting certainly got under the skin of the FBI
brass. Here was Castro, one of America's major enemies—a
revolutionary who was aligned with the Soviets—trying to
garner the favor of Malcolm X, the highly influential leader
of "angry" anti-American black citizens. At the time, the FBI
was trying to suppress both Communist influences and black
"troublemakers," and now the two were seemingly joining
forces. Soon after this meeting, FBI special agents were
attending all of Malcolm's speeches.

They must have watched with jaws dropped in December
1962, when Malcolm delivered a 14,000-word speech
centered on the fable of Yakub—one of the first of Malcolm's

speeches for which transcripts exist. By this time, tensions were increasing between Malcolm and Elijah Muhammad, yet he still taught the message of the NOI leader—as bizarre as it could sometimes be. Here is an excerpt of that December speech:

"The Honorable Elijah Muhammad says that the white man went down into the caves of Europe and he lived there for two thousand years on all fours. . . . Hair grew all over their bodies. By being on all fours, the end of their spine began to grow. They grew a little tail that came out from the end of their spine. . . . And just like a dog, he was crawling around up there. He was hairy as a dog. He had a tail like a dog. He had a smell like a dog. . . .

The Honorable Elijah Muhammad says that all the beasts up in Europe wanted to kill the white man. . . . They hated the white man. So, he says, what the white man would do, he'd dig a hole in the hill, that was his cave. . . . He'd sit outside of the cave at night in a tree with rocks in his hand, and if any beast came up and tried to get in the cave at his family, he'd throw rocks at it, or he'd have a club that he'd swing down and try to drive it away with it."

While few people heard Malcolm's NOI addresses, he often spoke to the media about the race issues of the day. Malcolm was furious in April 1962 when a simple incident resulted in tragedy. In Los Angeles, unarmed Nation of Islam members were pulled over by police on the night of April 27 because they had a lot of clothing in their car. Once out of the car, one of the men started talking with his hands, causing the police to restrain him. Another officer fired a shot, resulting in an all-call to officers in the area. Dozens of officers arrived, but they focused their attention on the NOI mosque nearby. Police fired on the mosque for no apparent reason, wounding six unarmed Muslims and killing unarmed Ronald Stokes. Newspapers pictured Stokes handcuffed, face down, lying in a puddle of his own blood.

"Seven Muslims were shot," Malcolm told New York radio station WBAI. "None of them were armed. None of them were struggling. None of them were fighting. None of them were trying to defend themselves at all. . . . And this happened in Los Angeles last Friday night, in the United States of America—not South Africa or France or Portugal or any place else or in Russia behind the iron curtain, but right here in the United States of America."

The incident fanned the flames of black anger in Los Angeles, which would continue to burn until the explosive Watts riot in 1965.

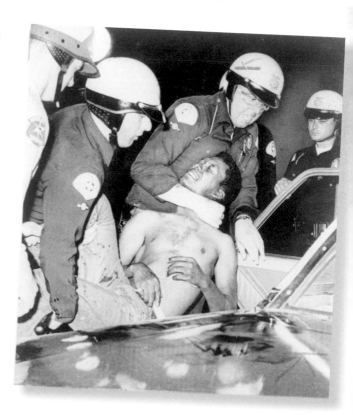

Watts riot in 1965

By 1963, Malcolm was a national figure, though not nearly as well-known as Martin Luther King Jr. In May, King led a desegregation movement in Birmingham, Alabama, that included the "children's crusade"—the march of young African Americans to city hall. The nation watched aghast as police officers and firefighters unleashed attack dogs and powerful fire hoses—strong enough to break a person's ribs—on the teenage demonstrators. Malcolm X criticized the activists' tactics in Birmingham, stating that "real men don't put their children on the firing line." Nevertheless, the campaign achieved its purpose: Many U.S. citizens and members of Congress became fed up with Jim Crow and called for the passage of legislation to end segregation.

Throughout the mid-1960s, civil rights activists staged hundreds of sit-ins, read-ins (at segregated libraries), wade-ins (pools and beaches), kneel-ins (churches), and all kinds of "ins" in their efforts to destroy Jim Crow. Thousands were arrested, harassed, assaulted, expelled from school, fired from their jobs, evicted from their homes, and even killed despite following the nonviolent tactics of the movement. Malcolm lauded the courage of the participants, but he ridiculed the movement as a whole.

"I can't turn around without hearing about some 'civil rights advance'!" he wrote. "White people seem to think the black man ought to be shouting 'hallelujah'! Four hundred years the white man has had his foot-long knife in the black man's back. . . ." Or as he stated on another occasion, "An integrated cup of coffee isn't sufficient pay for four hundred years of slave labor."

A student being carried out in the chair she
was sitting in to protest segregation

Throughout the civil rights movement, Malcolm told it "like it is," as people used to say in the '60s. While King made Americans feel good with his "table of brotherhood" optimism, Malcolm painted a starker picture.

"[T]here is plenty wrong with Negroes," he told Alex Haley in his famous *Playboy* magazine interview in early 1963. "They have no society. They're robots, automatons. No minds of their own. I hate to say that about us, but it's the truth. They are a black body with a white brain. Like the monster Frankenstein." At the bottom of the social heap, he said "is the black man in the big-city ghetto. He lives night and day with the rats and cockroaches and drowns himself with alcohol and anesthetizes himself with dope, to try and forget where and what he is. That Negro has given up all hope."

When Haley asked him why he had called it "good news" that 120 white Atlantans had died in a plane crash, Malcolm said:

"The white man has reveled as the rope snapped black men's necks. He has reveled around the lynching fire. It's only right for the black man's true God, Allah, to defend us—and for us to be joyous because our God manifests his ability to inflict pain on our enemy. We Muslims believe that the white race, which is guilty of having oppressed and exploited and enslaved our people here in America, should and will be the victims of God's divine wrath."

To many whites and some blacks, Malcolm's fiery comments often seemed to be destructively negative. He even rained on the parade of the historic March on Washington in August 1963, when Martin Luther King Jr. delivered his inspiring and uniting "I Have a Dream" speech. Witnessing what he called the "Farce on Washington," Malcolm was disgusted by the watered-down speeches and "picnic" atmosphere.

> "I observed that circus," he wrote. "Who ever heard of angry revolutionists all harmonizing 'We Shall Overcome . . . Suum Day . . .' while tripping and swaying along arm-in-arm with the very people they were supposed to be angrily revolting against?"

While Malcolm consistently railed against the white race, his relationship with his beloved mentor, Elijah Muhammad, was becoming increasingly strained. The resulting schism between the two men would shake Malcolm to the core and lead him on an entirely new path.

View of the 1963 March on Washington

Malcolm speaking at
a Harlem rally, 1963

6 THE TRANSFORMATION

THE ASSASSINATION of President John F. Kennedy on November 22, 1963, paralyzed the nation. The young, charismatic president had energized the country, and in a blink he was gone. Americans were stunned for days, in mourning for weeks.

Elijah Muhammad, whose Nation of Islam ministers had routinely criticized America's white power structure, knew that this was not the time to say anything disparaging about the slain president. Just hours after Kennedy was shot dead, Muhammad ordered his ministers not to comment on the assassination. Unfortunately, it was not easy keeping a zipper on the lips of Malcolm X. On December 1, 1963, shortly after Malcolm spoke at the Manhattan Center in New York, someone asked him what he thought of the assassination.

"Without a second thought," Malcolm later wrote, "I said what I honestly felt—that it was, as I saw it, a case of 'the chickens coming home to roost.' I said that the hate in white men had not stopped with the killing of defenseless black people, but that hate, allowed to spread unchecked, finally had struck down this country's Chief of State."

Not surprisingly, Malcolm's quote was all over the news media. Here was an angry black man, working for an organization that many considered a hate group, saying something that seemed disrespectful about the slain president.

Muhammad knew this was a horrible public-relations blow to the NOI. The next day, during a scheduled meeting with Malcolm, Muhammad met him with an embrace, like he always had. But this time, Malcolm felt the messenger's tension.

"Did you see the papers this morning?" Muhammad asked.

"Yes, sir, I did," Malcolm replied.

"That was a very bad statement," Muhammad said. "The country loved this man. The whole country is in mourning. That was very ill-timed. A statement like that can make it hard on Muslims in general."

Muhammad told Malcolm that he was not allowed to speak publicly for ninety days. Malcolm was numb. He had always enjoyed a warm relationship with his beloved mentor, and now he was being punished.

But that wasn't the half of it. According to Malcolm, he wasn't just being punished; he was being manipulated.

Soon after Malcolm's meeting with Muhammad, the Nation of Islam sent telegrams to the New York media, informing them that Malcolm X had been suspended for three months. After that, NOI members were notified that Malcolm would be reinstated after ninety days "if he submits." Now Malcolm was getting suspicious. Always respectful of Muhammad, Malcolm had told him that he would honor the suspension. But "if he submits" made it sound as if he was a troublemaker.

Malcolm also learned that, during the suspension, he would not be allowed to teach in his own Temple Seven in New York. And days later, a poisonous rumor reached his ears. "If you

Malcolm deconstructing the term "negro" during
a sermon at Temple 7 in August 1963

knew what the minister [Malcolm] did," a Temple Seven official was telling some fellow members, "you'd go out and kill him yourself."

"And then I knew," Malcolm wrote. "As any official in the Nation of Islam would instantly have known, any death-talk for me could have been approved of—if not actually initiated—by only one man."

Elijah Muhammad.

The rift between the NOI leader and his most popular minister had actually begun months before the Kennedy assassination. For years, Malcolm had heard ugly rumors about Muhammad's marital infidelity. He ignored them, thinking that no one was of higher moral character than his beloved "prophet." But by the summer of 1963, the rumors hardened into fact. On July 3, United Press International reported that Muhammad, age sixty-seven, was facing paternity suits from two former secretaries, both in their twenties, who claimed that Muhammad had fathered their children. One woman had bore one of the children, while the other woman had given birth to two and was pregnant with a third.

Fearing that the claims were true, Malcolm approached Muhammad's son, Wallace, who didn't deny the reports. Then Malcolm personally talked to three former secretaries of Muhammad, each of whom admitted to fathering their boss's children. They also shared with Malcolm what Muhammad had told them about him—that Malcolm would leave the NOI someday and that he was "dangerous." "I learned from these former secretaries of Mr. Muhammad that while he was praising me to my face, he was tearing me apart behind my back," Malcolm wrote.

In April 1963, Muhammad invited Malcolm to visit him in Phoenix, Arizona, where he all but admitted his indiscretions. "When you read about how David took another man's wife, I'm that David," Muhammad said. "You read about Noah, who got drunk—that's me. You read about Lot, who went and laid up with his own daughters. I have to fulfill all of those things." Muhammad's revelation shattered Malcolm's faith in his leader and the Nation of Islam.

Elijah Muhammad

Even before his post-assassination "silencing," Malcolm began talking less about religion and more about social issues and politics. During the suspension, he realized that the schism between the NOI leadership and him was irreparable and that his life was in danger.

The "death-talk" that Malcolm mentioned would haunt him the rest of his short life. But, he said, he did not live in fear. "I don't worry," he told reporters months later.

"I tell ya, I'm a man who believed that I died twenty years ago, and I live like a man who's dead already. I have no fear whatsoever of anybody or anything."

During his suspension, from December 1963 through February 1964, many began to realize that Malcolm would leave the Nation of Islam. Besides Muhammad's infidelity, another factor came into play—jealousy. When Muhammad learned that Malcolm was featured more than him in Louis Lomax's 1963 book *When the Word Is Given*, about the Nation of Islam, the NOI leader was reportedly upset. Moreover, some of the organization's leaders were not happy that Malcolm had become a larger figure than their leader.

Nation of Islam members were not supposed to attend sporting events, but the rule did not prevent Malcolm X from attending the Cassius Clay–Sonny Liston heavyweight championship bout on February 25, 1964. Clay and Malcolm had become close friends, and at the time they may have been the most outspoken black celebrities the nation had ever known. The two men prayed together before the fight, and then Clay went out and knocked out the "unbeatable" Sonny Liston in one of the most spectacular upsets in sports history. "I shook

Malcolm and Ali in New York on March 1, 1964

up the world!" Clay said afterward. The next morning, Clay announced that he had committed himself to Islam. Forevermore, he would be known as Muhammad Ali.

Ironically, Malcolm X was on the verge of leaving the Nation of Islam. On March 8, 1964, he issued a statement that made it official. Though he said he would remain a Muslim, he declared that the Black Muslim movement had "gone as far as it can" because it was too inhibited and too narrowly sectarian. He said he was "prepared to cooperate in local civil-rights actions in the South and elsewhere. . . . Good education, housing, and jobs are imperatives for the Negroes, and I shall support them in their fight to win these objectives." The statement did not condemn the Nation of Islam, Elijah Muhammad, or any NOI members.

On March 12, Malcolm X issued a prepared statement and held a press conference in New York City to more fully explain his intentions. For one thing, he was backing off the NOI claim that "separation" from the white race was the only solution for black Americans. He said that a return to Africa or the creation of a separate nation was "the best solution," but he admitted that it was "still a long-range program."

In this statement, Malcolm announced his intention to form his own organization, Muslim Mosque, Inc. He declared at the press conference:

"It will be the working base for an action program designed to eliminate the political oppression, the economic exploitation, and the social degradation suffered daily by twenty-two million Afro-Americans."

In an important development in the civil rights movement, Malcolm declared on March 12:

"We must find a common approach, a common solution to a common problem. As of this minute, I've forgotten everything bad that the other leaders have said about me, and I pray they can also forget the many bad things I've said about them."

That comment came at an appropriate time, because just fourteen days later Malcolm would meet Martin Luther King for the first and only time in their lives. The two men met in Washington, where they both came to hear the Senate debate on the Civil Rights Bill that was pending in Congress. The meeting was fleeting—approximately one minute—but cordial. Photographers captured the two men shaking hands and beaming broadly.

Not long after his March 12 announcement, Malcolm visited his half-sister Ella in Boston, telling her that he wanted to make a pilgrimage to Mecca, the sacred birthplace of the prophet Muhammad. This intention is noteworthy, because it shows that he was committed to Islam—despite the social

Malcolm and Martin Luther King Jr. on March 26, 1964

and political aims of his new organization—and that he had made a clean break from the NOI. Very few of the Nation's members had ever made a pilgrimage to Mecca. Ella gave him money for his trip.

Malcolm X and his family would leave for Mecca on April 13. But before they did, Malcolm delivered what American Rhetoric.com rates as the seventh-greatest speech in American history—his "The Ballot or the Bullet" speech at Cory Methodist Church in Cleveland, Ohio, on April 3, 1964. The meeting was sponsored by the local chapter of the Congress of Racial Equality (CORE), which is significant because CORE was a major mainstream civil rights organization—one that cosponsored the March on Washington. This shows that Malcolm was becoming immersed in the movement that he had so strongly denounced.

Unlike his many speeches of previous years, in which he spoke in the name of the prophet Elijah Muhammad, this speech was pure Malcolm. It was political, centering on the Civil Rights Bill that was still pending in Congress and which southern Democrats were trying to defeat. As gleaned from the phrase "Ballot or the Bullet," it was threatening in nature. As such, it resonated with the small but growing "militant" faction of the civil rights movement, which was tiring of the baby-steps progress of the nonviolent movement and wanted action now.

Throughout the speech, Malcolm professed his disdain for and distrust of the government, which at the time was dominated by white men at every level. He said that 1964 was an election year, "when all of the white political crooks will be right back in your and my community . . . with their false promises which they don't intend to keep." While mainstream civil rights leaders were hoping that Washington would fix the ills of the segregated South, Malcolm expressed skepticism: "When you take your case to Washington, D.C., you're taking it to the criminal who's responsible; it's like running from the wolf to the fox. They're all in cahoots together."

Nevertheless, Malcolm declared that it was important for black citizens to vote.

"[W]hen white people are evenly divided," he said, "and black people have a bloc of votes of their own, it is left up to them to determine who's going to sit in the White House and who's going to be in the dog house."

At times during the speech, Malcolm was as inspiring as Martin Luther King. "You let that white man know," he said, "if this is a country of freedom, let it be a country of freedom; and if it's not a country of freedom, change it."

Malcolm made listeners rethink the civil rights movement. He said that the oppression of black Americans was a human rights issue and worthy of consideration by the United Nations (which was responsible for protecting human rights of mistreated peoples throughout the world). "Civil rights keeps you under [Uncle Sam's] restrictions, under his jurisdiction," Malcolm said. "Civil rights keeps you in his pocket. Civil rights means you're asking Uncle Sam to treat you right. Human rights are something you were born with. Human rights are your God-given rights. Human rights are the rights that are recognized by all nations of this earth. And any time anyone violates your human rights, you can take them to the world court."

Despite such insights, the seemingly threatening aspects of the speech earned the most press at the time. Malcolm said that black people should not "get a rifle and form battalions and go out looking for white folks . . . that would be illegal and we don't do anything illegal." He said, "I'm nonviolent with those who are nonviolent with me. But when you drop that violence on me, then you've made me go insane, and I'm not responsible for what I do."

Malcolm had been under the surveillance of the FBI, and he knew it, but it didn't prevent him from making strong, just-short-of-threatening demands of the president of the United States:

"Lyndon B. Johnson is the head of the Democratic Party. If he's for civil rights, let him go into the Senate next week and . . . denounce the southern branch of his party. Let him go in there right now and take a moral stand—right now, not later. Tell him, don't wait until election time. If he waits too long . . . he will be responsible for letting a condition develop in this country which will create a climate that will bring seeds up out of the ground with vegetation on the end of them looking like something these people never dreamed of. In 1964, it's the ballot or the bullet."

Malcolm X, whose life had metamorphosed several times already, was about to experience another transformation. As he made his pilgrimage with his family in April 1964, Malcolm went through a number of experiences that would change his world view. In his stop in Frankfurt, Germany, he was surprised how friendly the local people were. He spent two days with his family in Cairo, Egypt—sightseeing,

Malcolm meets with Prince (later king) Faisal al-Saud, the regent of Saudi Arabia during a pilgrimage to the Muslim holy city of Mecca.

reflecting—before arriving in Mecca. Dressed in white, thousands of fellow Muslims, of various nationalities, joined Malcolm in the pilgrimage. They chanted Islamic prayers and practiced rituals that Malcolm—the famous Nation of Islam minister—did not know.

Those who hosted Malcolm and his family were Muslims, but they were also white. He wrote to his assistants in Harlem, "Never have I witnessed such sincere hospitality and overwhelming spirit of true brotherhood as is practiced by people of all colors and races here in this ancient Holy Land. . . ." He added:

"There were tens of thousands of pilgrims, from all over the world. They were of all colors, from blue-eyed blonds to black-skinned Africans. But we were all participating in the same ritual, displaying a spirit of unity and brotherhood that my experiences in America had led me to believe never could exist between the white and the non-white. . . . I have never before seen sincere and true brotherhood practiced by all colors together, irrespective of their color."

To Malcolm, it became clear that the notion of whites as "blue-eyed devils"—as preached by the Nation of Islam—was erroneous. White racism was still prevalent in the United States and elsewhere, but Malcolm realized that good lay in all men and women, despite their race. "[O]n this pilgrimage, what I have seen, and experienced, has forced me to *re-arrange* much of my thought-patterns previously held, and to *toss aside* some of my previous conclusions," he wrote.

When Malcolm X returned from his pilgrimage in May 1964, he had a new name: El-Hajj Malik el-Shabazz. In his book *Message to the Blackman in America*, Elijah Muhammad had written that black people descended from the ancient tribe Shabazz. Malcolm's wife and children permanently adopted the new surname as well. Despite the name change, Malcolm was still popularly known as Malcolm X.

Alex Haley, the writer who had interviewed Malcolm for the 1963 *Playboy* article, was helping him write an autobiography. On May 21, 1964, the day that Malcolm arrived home from his trip, Haley took him to a press conference at the Hotel Theresa in Harlem. Haley recalled Malcolm's boyish smile and new, reddish beard. He also recalled the exchange he had with reporters.

"Do we correctly understand that you now do not think that all whites are evil?" a reporter asked.

"*True*, sir!" Malcolm replied. "My trip to Mecca has opened my eyes. I no longer subscribe to racism. I have adjusted my thinking to the point where I believe that whites are human beings . . . as long as this is borne out by their humane attitude toward Negroes." Malcolm continued: "I'm *not* a racist. I'm not condemning whites for being whites. . . . I condemn what whites collectively have done to our people collectively."

On June 28 at New York's Audubon Ballroom, Malcolm announced the formation of the Organization of Afro-American Unity. Extraordinarily ambitious, the OAAU hoped to unify and help not only African Americans but everyone of African descent. On the home front, Malcolm said, the organization would address such civil rights issues as voter registration and school improvements. But he also stressed the importance of *human* rights issues. The OAAU aimed to create social programs that would help black addicts, unwed mothers, and children in need.

That very summer, the major civil rights organizations were conducting the Mississippi Summer Project, aka Freedom Summer. Besides registering black voters (amid violent white reprisals), the activists established Freedom Schools to educate black students. In addition to being taught such basics as reading, writing, and math, the students learned about black history and a less "whitewashed" version of American history. The goals were to present *true* history and to give black students a feeling of pride in themselves and their heritage.

This was revolutionary education at the time, but the OAAU aimed to do the same thing. Malcolm, who wrote about how his teacher used to laugh at blacks' supposed lack of contributions to history, aimed to correct such injustice. A stated mission of the OAAU was to "devise original educational methods and procedures which will liberate the minds of our children from the vicious lies and distortions that are fed to us from the cradle to keep us mentally enslaved. We will . . . encourage qualified Afro-Americans to write and publish the textbooks needed to liberate our minds."

In addition to helping African Americans, the OAAU aimed for unity among all people of African descent. Malcolm believed in Pan-Africanism—uniting all African descendants

into an African community. On a more practical level, the
OAAU wanted to create a "technician bank," a group of skilled
African Americans who could help their poorer brothers and
sisters in Africa.

Malcolm in Cairo in July 1, 1964, pointing out quotations in the Qur'an

Excited by his bold, new mission, Malcolm returned to Africa
in July 1964 and attended the Organization of African Unity
in Cairo. The only American at the conference, he submitted a
paper that asked the delegates to consider the plight of oppressed
African Americans. African leaders liked how Malcolm, as a
representative of black Americans, was reaching out to them.
Malcolm spoke to large gatherings. He met with Jomo Kenyatta,
who would become president of Kenya later in 1964. He also
conferred with Milton Obote, the prime minister of Uganda. By
October, Malcolm had met with eleven heads of state in Africa.

When Malcolm returned to the United States on November
24, 1964, he immediately held a press conference. The United
States, he declared, had violated the human rights of black

citizens, and he had gathered support for an appeal to the United Nations on behalf of black Americans. In the eyes of some Americans, such an action was borderline treasonous. The FBI was watching Malcolm, and they had the power to destroy his career—just like they would cripple the Black Panthers later in the decade.

Malcolm spoke frequently in 1964 and early 1965. He often talked on college campuses, and he addressed members of both the OAAU and Muslim Mosque, Inc. Major magazines, such as the *Saturday Evening Post*, published stories about this extraordinary man with the bold, revolutionary rhetoric.

More and more black Americans began to embrace Malcolm's teachings. Many had become disillusioned with the nonviolent civil rights movement and were looking for more direct action. This was especially true in America's big cities, where black citizens were becoming increasingly fed up with the brutality of white police officers, oppressive living conditions, and

A stained-glass window in Sage Chapel at Cornell University, honoring three slain civil rights activists, James Chaney, Andrew Goodman, and Michael Schwerner

pervasive job discrimination. In the South, civil rights activists were doubting the effectiveness of King's movement. A church bombing in Birmingham, Alabama, in September 1963 killed four black girls. In Mississippi, reprisals to Freedom Summer left four activists dead, eighty beaten, a thousand arrested, and more than sixty churches, homes, and businesses burned or bombed.

Civil rights activists didn't have to move too far to the left to find equal ground with Malcolm, who was becoming more and more mainstream. An OAAU statement in February 1965 indicated that Malcolm was more willing than ever to work with whites.

"We Afro-Americans feel receptive toward all peoples of goodwill," the statement read. "We are not opposed to multi-ethnic associations in any walk of life. In fact, we have had experiences which enable us to understand how unfortunate it is that human beings have been set apart or aside from each other because of characteristics known as 'racial' characteristics."

Yet in his final weeks of life, Malcolm had not lost any of his assertiveness. In early 1965, while Martin Luther King was in jail in Selma, Alabama, during the pivotal voting-rights campaign in that city, Malcolm traveled to Selma and met with King's wife, Coretta Scott King. "I didn't come to Selma to make his job difficult," he told Coretta. "I really did come thinking that I could make it easier. If the white people realize what the alternative is, perhaps they will be more willing to hear Dr. King."

In early 1965, Malcolm was only thirty-nine years old. His appeal was so vast, his goals so immense, and his determination so strong that his new organizations had the potential to change the world in extraordinary ways. But he didn't get the chance. By February, he was a dead man walking.

7
THE ASSASSINATION

Malcolm X and his family escaped unharmed after two Molotov cocktails sparked a flash fire at his home.

ON FEBRUARY 14, 1965, Malcolm and his wife Betty, who was pregnant, and their four daughters were sleeping peacefully in their house in Queens, New York. But at a quarter to three that morning, a frightening blast awakened them. Someone had thrown a gasoline bomb through their picture window, and the house was on fire. Grabbing the children, Malcolm and Betty frantically led them out the back door and into the yard. All were unharmed, but half the house would be destroyed before firefighters could douse the flames.

A day later in a speech at New York's Audubon Ballroom, Malcolm insisted he knew who the culprit was. "My house was bombed by the *Muslims*!" he said.

Malcolm had every reason to believe that Black Muslims (Nation of Islam members) were trying to kill him. Elijah Muhammad reportedly told one of his ministers, while referring to Malcolm, "With these hypocrites, when you find them, cut their heads off." The next month, an issue of the NOI newspaper, *Muhammad Speaks*, included a cartoon of Malcolm's severed head. In December 1964, NOI minister Louis X said that "such a man as Malcolm is worthy of death." Malcolm received death threats at his home, and the FBI—which had put Malcolm under surveillance— had also recorded death threats.

"Why are they threatening your life?" a reporter asked Malcolm. He replied:

"Well, primarily because they are afraid that I will tell the real reason that I am out of the Black Muslim movement—which I never told; I kept it to myself. But the real reason is that Elijah Muhammad, the head of the movement, is the father of eight children by six different teenage girls who were his private, personal secretaries. The one who first made me aware of this was Wallace Muhammad, Mr. Muhammad's son. . . . On a program in Chicago called *Hotline*, moderated by Wesley South, John Ali, the national secretary, admitted—I think it was Wednesday or Thursday, one of those days last week—that they were absolutely going to kill me."

Malcolm said in that interview that he owned a rifle and that he intended to use it if someone came to his house without a good reason. A famous photograph documents that Malcolm owned an automatic rifle. In the photo, he holds the weapon upright with his right hand while peering through his curtains.

The firebombing of Malcolm's house seemed to have the Nation of Islam's fingerprints all over it. Months earlier, the NOI had sued to reclaim the house from Malcolm, claiming they owned it. They won the case, and Malcolm and his family were ordered to vacate the premises. A hearing had been scheduled for February 14 to postpone the eviction date. The bomb smashed through the picture window just hours before that scheduled hearing.

Malcolm answers reporters' questions at the Audubon Ballroom in New York City on February 15, 1965.

Betty and the girls went to stay with friends, while a clearly distraught Malcolm tried to continue his normal schedule. He flew to Detroit to deliver a scheduled speech, then returned to New York for a speech on Monday night (February 15) at the Audubon Ballroom, where he declared that Black Muslims had tried to kill him.

"I have been marked for death in the next five days," he said. "I have the names of five Black Muslims who have been chosen to kill me."

On Friday, Malcolm granted an interview to *Life* magazine writer/photographer Gordon Parks, who asked him about an incident from years earlier. A young white woman had asked him what she could do to help end racism. He told her nothing, and she left in tears.

"Well, I've lived to regret that incident," Malcolm said. "In many parts of the African continent I saw white students helping black people. Something like this kills a lot of argument. I did many things as a [Black] Muslim that I'm sorry for now. I was a zombie then—like all [Black] Muslims—I was hypnotized, pointed in a certain direction and told to march. Well, I guess a man's entitled to make a fool of himself if he's ready to pay the cost. It cost me twelve years."

Malcolm also told Parks, "The sickness and madness of those days—I'm glad to be free of them. It is a time for martyrs now, and if I am to be one, it will be for the cause of brotherhood. That's the only thing that can save this country. I've learned it the hard way—but I've learned it. And that's the significant thing."

The next day, Saturday, Malcolm and Betty found a house they wanted to buy on Long Island. He called Haley that afternoon, asking him if the publisher of his autobiography could advance him $4,000 so he could buy a new house; he had only $150 to his name. Haley said he'd ask the publisher about it on Monday morning. For Malcolm, Monday would never come.

With a speech scheduled for Sunday, February 21, Malcolm spent Saturday night at the nearby Hilton Hotel.

His Sunday began at 8 o'clock with an ominous phone call. "Wake up, brother," a man told Malcolm before hanging up. Perhaps sensing that he might never see his family again, Malcolm phoned Betty and asked her to change the family's plans—to come to the Audubon for his 2 o'clock speech. She agreed.

Audubon Ballroom

Malcolm normally exuded confidence and positive energy, but as he arrived at the Audubon in his dark suit he appeared agitated, anxious, worn out. He was short-tempered with a young female assistant, but he made sure to apologize, saying he was under great stress. People flooded into the ballroom, where some four hundred wooden chairs had been set up. As with all of Malcolm's speeches, no guests were checked for weapons; he wanted people to feel welcome.

Prior to Malcolm's address, Brother Benjamin X spoke for a half-hour. Malcolm then took the stage. "*Asalaikum,* brothers and sisters!" Malcolm said. Then came a disturbance from the gathering, about eight rows from the front. "Take your hand out of my pocket!" a man yelled. The incident caught the attention of the crowd, and Malcolm told the two feuding men to calm down.

It was all meant to be a distraction, for moments later two or three other men rushed toward the stage. One fired a shotgun at Malcolm, who was also hit by bullets from a handgun. Malcolm grabbed his chest and then fell backward, crashing on the floor. Those in the crowd screamed and took cover. Betty, hysterical, ran to the stage. "They're killing my husband!" she cried.

Police officers apprehended a man with a handgun, twenty-two-year-old Talmadge Hayer, as he tried to escape from the ballroom. They shoved him into their police car and drove away. Malcolm was rushed to the hospital, where he was soon pronounced dead.

A flurry of activity surrounded the hours and days after Malcolm's death. New York detectives jumped on the murder case, determined to find all those involved in this preplanned assassination. Police were on high alert in Harlem, fearing a potential riot (hundreds had been injured in a Harlem

Scenes from the shooting

uprising the year before). The big news in Harlem occurred at NOI's Temple Seven, which was set afire.

Meanwhile, arrangements were made at the Unity Funeral Home, and Malcolm's six-year-old daughter, Attallah, wrote her father a letter: "Dear Daddy, I love you so. O Dear O Dear I wish you wasn't dead."

Under pressure for his reaction, Elijah Muhammad offered this response: "Malcolm died according to his preaching. He seems to have taken weapons as his god. Therefore, we couldn't tolerate a man like that. He preached war. We preach peace."

From February 23 to 26, an estimated 20,000 people filed past Malcolm's casket. On the 27th, the funeral at the Faith Temple Church of God in Christ was broadcast on local television. Actor and civil rights activist Ossie Davis, who called Malcolm "our own black shining prince," delivered a poignant eulogy:

"They will say that he is of hate—a fanatic, a racist—who can only bring evil to the cause for which you struggle! And we will answer and say to them: Did you ever talk to Brother Malcolm? Did you ever touch him or have him smile at you? Did you ever really listen to him? Did he ever do a mean thing? Was he ever himself associated with violence or any public disturbance? For if you did, you would know him. And if you knew him, you would know why we must honor him."

Newspapers in Ghana and Nigeria each referred to Malcolm as a martyr. Martin Luther King Jr. wrote the following in a telegram to Betty: "While we did not always see eye to eye on methods to solve the race problem, I always

Islamic prayers are chanted at the grave site of Malcolm X, as his widow, Betty, looks on in silence.

had a deep affection for Malcolm and felt that he had a great ability to put his finger on the existence and root of the problem. He was an eloquent spokesman for his point of view and no one can honestly doubt that Malcolm had a great concern for the problems that we face as a race."

For two weeks after Malcolm's murder, Betty Shabazz suffered from nightmares of the assassination. Waking hours were horrific, too. She had no money, no home, and four daughters to care for, and she was pregnant with twins. Actor Ruby Dee and Juanita Poitier (wife of famed actor Sidney Poitier) established a committee that held benefit concerts for Betty and her family. In death, Malcolm was able to help, too. *The Autobiography of Malcolm X*, published in 1965 by Grove Press, became an enormous best seller. Alex Haley split the royalties with Betty, which provided her with a steady income.

For months and years after the murder, Americans still wondered: Who killed Malcolm X? Talmadge Hayer certainly was one of the gunmen. At first he told police that he hadn't done it—that he had simply picked up the gun in the aftermath of the murder and decided to keep it. But he eventually admitted to shooting Malcolm. Hayer was affiliated with the Fruit of Islam, a paramilitary organization that

A first edition copy of the *Autobiography of Malcolm X*, published in 1965

protected the Nation of Islam. Hayer signed an affidavit saying that he had agreed with coconspirators to assassinate Malcolm X in the following fashion: A man would cause a disturbance in the crowd (the "hand out of my pocket" guy), and then Hayer and two others would rise and shoot Malcolm.

Days after the assassination, police arrested Nation of Islam "enforcers" 3X Butler, age twenty-six, and Thomas 15 X, twenty-nine. Eyewitnesses identified the two men as being at the ballroom and involved in the killing. However, the two men denied their involvement, and Hayer also said that they weren't involved. Others claimed that OAAU members were well aware of the two men, and if the pair had shown up at the ballroom that day, they would have been recognized as hostile members. Despite no conclusive evidence regarding these two men, they along with Hayer were all found guilty of first-degree murder on March 11, 1966. A month later, they were each sentenced to life in prison.

As with many high-profile assassinations, conspiracy theories arose. Some conspirators have pointed a finger at the Italian Mafia. They claim that the Mafia didn't like how Malcolm had convinced many Harlemites to stay away from drugs, which was a source of income for many in the mob.

Another theory is that the FBI was involved in the murder. That organization, run by J. Edgar Hoover, had been following Malcolm for years and had files on him that totaled more than 3,600 pages. The FBI's counterintelligence program (COINTELPRO)

J. Edgar Hoover

was designed to monitor, infiltrate, discredit, and disrupt domestic political organizations and individuals. Hoover wanted to prevent the rise of a black "messiah"—one who would lead a large-scale revolt of oppressed African Americans against white America. Hoover thought that several men could be that messiah, including Martin Luther King Jr., Elijah Muhammad, Stokely Carmichael, and Malcolm X. When civil rights activist Viola Liuzzo was shot to death by a small group of whites in Alabama in March 1965, it was discovered that one of the whites was an FBI informant.

The FBI would conspire with police departments in numerous raids of the Black Panthers, an organization with an agenda similar to Malcolm's. In 1969, the FBI assisted the Chicago police in bringing down Fred Hampton, a Panthers leader. Police raided Hampton's home and shot him to death. No one has proven that the FBI was directly involved in the murder of Malcolm X, but many conspiracy theorists believe that Hoover's men were somehow complicit in the crime.

Historians believe that Hayer was not the only NOI member involved in the assassination. Many feel that Louis X (later known as Louis Farrakhan) played a role. He had said in 1964 that "such a man as Malcolm is worthy of death." After the assassination, Elijah Muhammad promoted Louis X to two of Malcolm's former roles: national spokesman of the NOI and minister of the Harlem Temple.

In 1994, Qubilah Shabazz was asked if Farrakhan—who in 1975 became the leader of the NOI—was somehow involved in her father's murder. "Of course, yes," she said. "Nobody kept it a secret. It was a badge of honor. Everybody talked about it, yes." On *60 Minutes* in 2009, Farrakhan all but admitted that his rhetoric contributed to the murder. "I may have been complicit in words that I spoke leading up to February 21 [1965]," Farrakhan said. "I acknowledge that and regret that any word that I have said caused the loss of life of a human being."

Sadly, the tragedy that pervaded Malcolm's life—including the death of his father and his mother's loss of sanity—did not end with his assassination. In 1997, Malcolm's twelve-year-old grandson, Malcolm Shabazz, was suffering from serious mental health problems. On June 1, he poured gasoline in the apartment of his grandmother, Betty Shabazz, then started a fire. Malcolm X's widow suffered burns on 80 percent of her body.

Compounding the tragedy, Betty apparently could have avoided the flames by escaping through another part of the apartment. But she thought "I was stuck," a remorseful Malcolm Shabazz said years later, "and she had to run and get me."

Three weeks after the fire, Betty Shabazz died from her injuries.

A handcuffed Malcolm Shabazz

Malcolm X statue in the lobby
of the Malcolm X and Dr.
Betty Shabazz Memorial and
Educational Center in Harlem

8
THE LEGACY OF MALCOLM X

FROM THE EARLY TO MID-1960S, African Americans' attitudes toward civil rights began to change. Thanks to tell-it-like-it-is preachers and writers like Malcolm X, black citizens had become more aware of America's racial injustices, and many fumed with anger. They also had seen that white America's closed door would budge if pushed, and many wanted to smash the whole thing down.

Sam Cooke's 1964 song "A Change Is Gonna Come" became a black-activist anthem. And as African American author James Baldwin wrote in the prophetically titled 1963 book *The Fire Next Time*, "The Negroes of this country may never be able to rise to power, but they are very well placed indeed to precipitate chaos and ring down the curtain on the American dream."

Malcolm X's insightful and powerful rhetoric deeply affected African Americans. His message was printed in black newspapers and magazines as well as the growing number of books written by black authors in the 1960s. As a passionate and gifted writer and orator, Malcolm had delivered words that stuck with people. "We didn't land on Plymouth Rock," he said about black Americans. "The rock was landed on us!" Black citizens strongly related to such Malcolm comments as this: "I see America through the eyes of the victim. I don't see any American dream—I see an American nightmare."

In the mid- to late 1960s, *The Autobiography of Malcolm X* sold hundreds of thousands of copies each year. Black author David Bradley said that people didn't just read the autobiography; they were transformed by it. "[S]omehow that book . . . took hold of them," he wrote. "Got *inside* them. Altered their vision, their outlook, their insight. Changed their lives."

We must be careful not to make a direct connection, but Malcolm's near-militant language may have contributed to the race riots that erupted in America's large cities in the mid- to late 1960s. Julius Lester, in a 1966 article entitled "The Angry Children of Malcolm X," wrote:

"More than any other person Malcolm X was responsible for the new militancy that entered The Movement in 1965. Malcolm X said aloud those things which Negroes had been saying among themselves. He even said those things Negroes had been afraid to say to each other. His clear, uncomplicated words cut through the chains of black minds like a giant blow-torch."

H. Rap Brown

Malcolm did not necessarily approve of violence, but—as evidenced in the "Ballot or the Bullet" speech—he liked to put the threat of violence out there to make white America worried and vulnerable. "By any means necessary" is probably the quote most associated with Malcolm.

The race riots, or uprisings, had a profound effect on American society. Black Americans had been oppressed in ghettos for generations but had felt powerless to fight back. But a growing number of black activists—with Malcolm a pioneer in such efforts—riled up the black citizenry. H. Rap Brown was one such militant activist. "If America don't come around," he declared in 1966, "we're going to burn it down!" That same year, Stokely Carmichael announced, "We been saying freedom for six years and we ain't got nothin'. What we gonna start saying now is Black Power!"

"Black Power" became an anthem for young militants, and uprisings followed. While race riots were sporadic from 1964 to '66, they became an epidemic in 1967. Seventy-five major uprisings were documented that year, with more than half of the eighty-three related deaths occurring in Detroit in July 1967. In many large cities, race riots

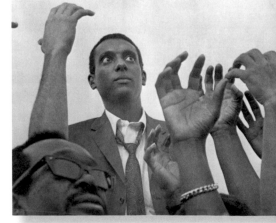

Stokely Carmichael

contributed significantly to "white flight." White citizens, upset by the unleashed anger of blacks in their cities, moved to the suburbs. Since whites in general had greater incomes than blacks, their departures left the cities with considerably less tax revenue. Detroit, Cleveland, St. Louis, and many other large cities became cash-strapped and rundown in the 1970s and beyond.

The connection from Malcolm X to black militancy to race riots to white flight to deteriorated cities is a tenuous one. However, his influence on the Black Power movement, which stretched from the mid-1960s to the 1970s, is undeniable.

Black militancy played a role in the Black Power movement, but the movement was more about empowering black Americans. Leaders tried to instill pride in African Americans—self-pride as well as pride in their culture and heritage. "Black Is Beautiful" became a popular catchphrase, and many black Americans wore hairstyles (such as the Afro) and clothing (including African garments) that reflected their true identity. The Black Arts movement (self-expression) and Black Studies movement (books and curricula that focused on African American history and other black-related issues) were subsets of the Black Power movement. Leaders of the movement also tried to get black Americans to work together to empower their communities. Moreover, the creation of the Congressional Black Caucus in 1969 was an outgrowth of the Black Power movement.

Many aspects of the Black Power movement reflected the teachings of Malcolm X, who had influenced many of the leaders of the movement.

Stokely Carmichael, who was the first to rally crowds with cries of "Black Power," has been called the "father" of the Black Power movement. Carmichael not only discussed Malcolm in great detail in his writings, but he did so in glowing terms. He remembered seeing one of Malcolm's speeches at Howard University. "Malcolm had a *presence*," Carmichael wrote. "It was

a noticeable life force, an energy field, an aura." He continued:
"[W]hat Malcolm demonstrated that night in Crampton
Auditorium on the Howard campus was the raw power, the
visceral potency, of the grip our unarticulated collective blackness
held over us." With each roar of the crowd, Carmichael recalled,
"the hairs tingled on the nape of my neck."

The Black Panthers, the most notable Black Power
organization, were strongly influenced by Malcolm X. Bobby
Seale, one of the Panthers' two co-founders, remembered the day
that his hero, Malcolm, was killed. Seale found a bunch of bricks
and broke them in half, then chucked them at every police car
that drove by. "I threw about half the bricks, and then I cried like
a baby," he wrote. He was so upset, he punched and smashed a
window of his mother's house. He vowed that day to "make my
own self into a [expletive] Malcolm X, and if they want to kill
me, they'll have to kill me." Referring to Eldridge Cleaver, one of
the three most prominent members of the Panthers, Seale wrote:
"Eldridge says Malcolm X had
an impact on everybody like
that, and Malcolm had that
impact on me."

Huey Newton, the other co-
founder of the Black Panthers,
wrote that "the Black Panther
Party exists in the spirit of
Malcolm X" and that "the
party is a living testament to
his life work. . . . Malcolm's
spirit is in us."

If that were the case, then
Malcolm had a spiritual hand
in the events of May 2, 1967,
in Sacramento, California.

Huey P. Newton and
Bobby Seale holding shotguns

Armed members of the Black Panther Party leaving the capitol in Sacramento, California

That was the day that Seale led thirty Black Panthers—twenty of them legally armed—to the state capitol. Many people, including Governor Ronald Reagan, scattered, and the Panthers instilled fear into the white Americans who later watched the events on television. The Panthers were trying to make a statement, for they were tired of seeing police officers intimidate and often brutalize unarmed citizens in black communities.

The Panthers unveiled a ten-point program, the first of which stated, "We want freedom. We want power to determine the destiny of our Black Community." They also wanted an end to police brutality, job discrimination, and whitewashed education. Other demands included decent housing, juries of black peers, and exemptions from military service for black Americans. (At the time, thousands of young Americans—including a disproportionate number of African Americans—were being drafted and sent to war in Vietnam.)

In the spirit of Malcolm X, the Panthers helped those in black communities with such programs as free health clinics and free breakfasts for impoverished children. They also ran "liberation schools" for young African Americans, and they ran petition campaigns for community control of police. Perhaps most notably, they put white Americans on edge. Images of the Panthers brandishing weapons and raising black-gloved fists as a show of black solidarity—again, reflections of Malcolm's teachings—made whites uneasy.

Richard Nixon in Philadelphia during his successful campaign to become president of the United States

In 1968, Richard Nixon ran for president on a law-and-order platform, promising to crack down on such rebellious "troublemakers" as antiwar protesters, rioters, and black militants. Nixon won with a sizable margin in the electoral vote but only a 0.7 percent edge in the popular vote—43.4 percent to 42.7 percent for Democrat Hubert Humphrey. If Malcolm X had lived a quiet life, afraid to voice his opinions, would Nixon have won the 1968 election? No one knows for sure, but if Nixon *had* lost, the United States would have been a much different nation in the 1970s and beyond.

Malcolm X's influence extended beyond the Black Power circle. Even John Lewis, one of the great civil rights leaders and a devoted follower of Martin Luther King's nonviolence philosophy, was affected. Recalled Carmichael, "Hey, after a long talk with Malcolm, even John Lewis had come back from Africa sounding like a Pan-Africanist revolutionary."

It's well known that the King-led civil rights movement had a strong effect on liberal white Americans. But later in the 1960s, as they read *The Autobiography of Malcolm X*, Americans of all races were transformed by Malcolm's worldview. "As a minority studying at college during the sixties, I heard a chorus of voices declaring their message regarding race relations, the Vietnam War, and

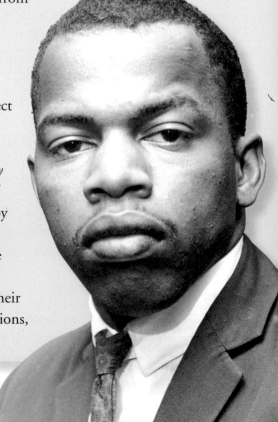

John Lewis

spiritual awakening," wrote author and religious scholar Jerry Yamamoto. "But one of the few voices that inspired me to seek peace in the world and within me was that of Malcolm X."

Even if Malcolm didn't have an effect on the 1968 presidential election, he did have a marked impact on 2008 presidential candidate Barack Obama. In *Dreams of My Father*, Obama wrote:

"Only Malcolm X's autobiography seemed to offer something different. His repeated acts of self-creation spoke to me; the blunt poetry of his words, his unadorned insistence on respect, promised a new and uncompromising order, martial in its discipline, forged through sheer force of will. All the other stuff, the talk of blue-eyed devils and apocalypse, was incidental to that program, I decided, religious baggage that Malcolm himself seemed to have safely abandoned toward the end of his life."

Malcolm X had such a powerful impact on his contemporaries that many vowed to keep the flame of his legacy burning. In the 1980s and beyond, educators, authors, musical artists, filmmakers, and even clothing manufacturers kept the spirit of Malcolm alive for future generations.

Though Malcolm had spent his life on the fringes of American society, that society—as it became more tolerant overall—became more accepting of him by the late 1960s. In 1968, residents in a predominantly black area of Chicago campaigned to have Herzl Junior College renamed after Malcolm. Their request was accepted, and in 1969 it was renamed Malcolm X College. There is nothing "separatist" about this two-year college. It has an open-admissions policy; anyone who wants to attend is welcome. Its stated mission is simply to empower "students of diverse backgrounds and abilities to achieve academic, career, and personal success."

In the 1980s, when drug use and violence were at an all-time high in America's inner cities, a Malcolm X resurgence took hold in African American communities. In 1981, a little-known actor named Denzel Washington played Malcolm X in the off-Broadway play *When the Chickens Came Home to Roost*. In 1986, the opera *X: The Life and Times of Malcolm X* was staged in New York City.

A big influence at the time was rap music, including the group Public Enemy. Chuck D, Flavor Flav, Terminator X, and the rest of Public Enemy instilled powerful social and political commentary in their lyrics. Their breakthrough album *It Takes a Nation of Millions to Hold Us Back* includes strong black-nationalist rhetoric. The track "Bring the Noise" even opens with a sample of a Malcolm X speech. "Too black, too strong," Malcolm declares. *It Takes a Nation* not only sold more than a million copies, but in 2003 *Rolling Stone* magazine hailed it as the most influential rap/hip-hop album of all time.

Public Enemy wasn't alone. According to the Center for Contemporary Black History at Columbia University, "Dozens of prominent performance artists within contemporary urban, 'hip hop culture,' began to draw upon the words and image of Malcolm X in their work."

In the 1980s and '90s, Malcolm X became an icon among the black youth of America. Like their parents had in the 1960s, these young African Americans identified with his message of self-respect and black pride. In one poll, 84 percent of African Americans age fifteen to twenty-four considered Malcolm "a hero for black Americans today."

Black youth began wearing baseball caps with just one symbol on them: the letter *X*. In fact, Malcolm X merchandise became an industry unto itself. Besides caps and T-shirts, companies churned out such products as Malcolm X air fresheners and even potato chips. *Baltimore Sun* columnist Mike Littwin, an admirer of Malcolm, thought the commercialization of his image was becoming ridiculous. "What's next?" he wrote in 1992. "Malcolm X World, the theme park? A tie-in with McDonald's where, if you purchase a Happy Meal, you can also buy an X-mobile?"

Filmmaker Spike Lee not only sold Malcolm X clothing in his Spike's Joint store, but in 1992 he paid homage to him with the film *Malcolm X*. Starring Denzel Washington, the film is a biography of his remarkable life, from youth to death. With a spellbinding performance by Washington and the masterful direction of Lee, *Malcolm X* inspired audiences and critics alike.

In the wake of the film, it became cool to like Malcolm X—and not just in African American communities. President Bill Clinton went jogging with a Malcolm X cap, and even some conservative Republicans jumped on the bandwagon. Recalled *The New Yorker*, "people as unlikely as Dan Quayle [U.S. vice president, 1989–93] talked sympathetically about Malcolm."

Malcolm's legacy lives on in a variety of ways. At 3448 Pinkney Street in Omaha, Nebraska, the Malcolm X House Site commemorates the place where he grew up. Besides Malcolm X College, dozens of schools are named after the African American icon. In the 1980s, streets in Harlem and Brooklyn were named Malcolm X Boulevard. Many other streets are named after him, too. A voracious reader, Malcolm would have been proud to attend the 1996 opening of the Malcolm X Library and Performing Arts Center in San Diego. Three years after that, the U.S. Postal Service issued the first Malcolm X stamps.

On May 19, Malcolm X Day is celebrated by individuals throughout the world. Since 1979 in Berkeley, California, the local government actually shuts down on Malcolm X Day, and schools are closed. Even though Berkeley has long been considered the "most liberal" city in America, shutting down for Malcolm X Day has not been without controversy. Many say that other historical figures are more worthy of such consideration. Others contend that Malcolm—who became a firm believer in self-discipline and education—would have preferred that students were in school learning. But when you consider that Berkeley has two unique day-off holidays—Malcolm X Day and International Women's Day—it shows that the city wants to recognize, in a special way, African Americans and women. It's hard to argue with their intentions.

In recent years, Americans have had more opportunities than ever to see and hear Malcolm X. Dozens of his speeches and interviews can be viewed on such Web sites as Hulu and YouTube. Through Netflix, you can quickly download and watch Spike Lee's *Malcolm X* as well as the documentaries *Malcolm Speaks* and *Malcolm X: A Search for Identity.*

With the death of Malcolm, society lost not only a great black leader but one who made all Americans think in different ways—to view life from a different perspective. If Malcolm X were alive today—during a time of economic duress, particularly for minorities and working-class Americans—he likely would be rallying the less privileged. If asked to comment on America's high poverty rate, rundown cities, and subpar inner-city schools, he likely would respond with loud and forceful rhetoric. After all, as he learned as a small child, "if you want something, you had better make some noise."

TIMELINE

1925
> Born Malcolm Little in Omaha, Nebraska, on May 19.

1931
> Father, black activist Earl Little, dies after getting hit by a streetcar on September 28.

1939
> Mother, Louise Little, is committed to a state mental institution in Michigan.

1941
> Moves to Boston, where he is enamored with the vibrancy of the black ghetto.

1943
> Moves to Harlem and becomes a waiter at Small's Paradise; gets involved in criminal activity; avoids military service by pretending to be crazy at the induction center.

1945
> Fearing for his life in Harlem, moves back to Boston, where he engages in house robberies with his friends and girlfriend.

1946
> Sentenced in Massachusetts to eight to ten years for larceny, breaking and entering, and carrying a weapon; begins serving time at Charlestown State Prison; reads voraciously while in prison.

1947
> Transferred to Concord Reformatory.

1948
> Transferred to the more humane Norfolk Prison Colony; becomes infatuated with the Nation of Islam (NOI).

1952
Released from prison on August 7; meets Elijah Muhammad several weeks later; changes his name to Malcolm X.

1953–55
Becomes minister of the Nation of Islam temples in Boston, Philadelphia, and New York; expands NOI membership with his recruiting skills and powerful speeches.

1957
Garners his first media attention after confronting police officers following the Johnson X Hinton altercation on April 26.

1958
Marries Betty Sanders on January 14; daughter Attallah, born on November 16—the first of six children.

1959
The Hate that Hate Produced, which airs on television in July, puts Malcolm and the Nation of Islam in the public eye; makes first trip to the Middle East and Africa.

1960
Meets with Cuban leader Fidel Castro in Harlem in September; second daughter, Qubilah, born.

1962
Third daughter, Ilyasah, is born.

1963
Loses faith in Elijah Muhammad after realizing that the NOI leader has fathered children with mistresses; criticizes the goals and tactics of the civil rights movement and calls the March on Washington the "Farce on Washington"; suspended by the Nation of Islam after referring to President Kennedy's November 22 assassination as a case of "the chickens coming home to roost."

1964

Announces in March his break from the Nation of Islam and the formation of Muslim Mosque, Inc.; meets Martin Luther King on March 26 for the first and only time; delivers his "The Ballot or the Bullet" speech on April 3; makes a pilgrimage to Mecca in the spring and returns with a softened view toward whites; changes his name to El-Hajj Malik el-Shabazz; announces the formation of the Organization of Afro-American Unity on June 28; meets with eleven heads of state in Africa by October; fourth daughter, Gamilah, born in December.

1965

House firebombed on February 14; shot to death during a speech at New York's Audubon Ballroom on February 21; *The Autobiography of Malcolm X* is published (millions of copies will be sold); twin daughters, Malaak and Malikah, born after his assassination.

1966

The Black Power movement, which is strongly influenced by the preachings of Malcolm X, begins in earnest.

1992

The popularity of the Spike Lee film *Malcolm X* coincides with a resurgence of interest in Malcolm.

1997

Betty Shabazz dies in a fire set by her grandson, Malcolm.

Sources

Chapter One: "Who Taught You to Hate Yourself?"

p. 12,   "Who taught you . . ." "Malcolm X: Who Taught You
           to Hate Yourself?" YouTube, http://www.youtube.com/
           watch?v=gRSgUTWffMQ.
p. 12,   "mm-hmm . . . that's right . . ." Ibid.
p. 12,   "Who taught you . . ." Ibid.
p. 12,   "You cannot be . . ." Ibid.
p. 13,   "They put *Moses* . . ." Ibid.
p. 13,   "They charged Jesus . . ." Ibid.
p. 14,   "Go to *those* . . ." Ibid.
p. 16,   "I feel that . . ." Alex Haley and Malcolm X, *The Autobiography of
           Malcolm X* (New York: Ballantine Books, 1990), 366–367.
p. 16,   "that's no realistic . . ." Ibid., 36.

Chapter Two: Black Child in a White World

p. 22,   "For the Negro . . ." Amy Jacques Garvey, *The Philosophy and
           Opinions of Marcus Garvey: Or, Africa for the Africans* (Dover,
           Mass.: The Majority Press, 1986), 53.
p. 24,   "by persons other . . ." Walter Dean Myers, *Malcolm X: By Any
           Means Necessary* (New York: Scholastic, 1993), 18.
p. 25,   "So early in . . ." Haley, *The Autobiography of Malcolm X*, 8.
p. 26,   "I remember how . . ." Ibid., 6–7.
p. 26,   "Man Run Over . . ." Myers, *Malcolm X*, 21.
p. 26,   "My father's skull . . ." Haley, *The Autobiography of Malcolm X*,
           10.
p. 27,   "how could my . . ." Ibid., 11.
p. 30,   "We children watched . . ." Ibid., 19.
p. 30,   "I truly believe . . ." Ibid., 21.
p. 33,   "I was unique . . ." Ibid., 31.
p. 35,   "Mr. Ostrowski looked . . ." Ibid., 36.

Chapter Three: Incarceration and Salvation

p. 37,   "That world of . . ." Haley, *The Autobiography of Malcolm X*, 42.
p. 41,   "Ella couldn't believe . . ." Ibid., 134.
p. 42,   "how bad, how . . ." Ibid., 150.
p. 44,   "Malcolm don't eat . . ." Ibid., 155.
p. 45,   "What do you . . ." Ibid., 159.
p. 46,   "You don't even . . ." Ibid., 161.
p. 48,   "It had an . . ." Ibid., 169.

SOURCES CONTINUED

Chapter Four: Empowering the NOI

p. 51, *"As-Salaam-Alaikum . . ."* Haley, *The Autobiography of Malcolm X*, 193.

p. 52, "Slavery, Suffering and . . ." Ibid., 195.

p. 55, "They asked if . . ." Ibid., 203.

p. 59, "sit down together . . ." "The I Have a Dream Speech," U.S. Constitution Online, http://www.usconstitution.net/dream.html.

p. 59, "We are against . . ." "Malcolm X Quotes," Malcolm X Online, http://www.malcolmxonline.com/malcolm-x-quotes.html.

p. 60, "[H]e was tall . . ." Karen S. Cole, "Sister Betty X Shabazz," Ezine Articles, http://ezinearticles.com/?Sister-Betty-X-Shabazz&id=613236.

p. 62, "You're not in . . ." "Malcolmology 101, #7: Johnson X Hinton," Malcolm X: A Life of Reinvention, http://www.malcolmxbio.com/node/15.

p. 63, "This is too . . ." Ibid.

Chapter Five: The National Stage

p. 65, "most powerful of . . ." Udo J. Hebel and Christoph Wagner, *Pictorial Cultures and Political Iconographies: Approaches, Perspectives, Case Studies from Europe and America* (Berlin: De Gruyter, 2011), 206.

p. 65, "liar . . . robber . . . drunkard . . ." Thomas David Jones, *Human Rights: Group Defamation, Freedom of Expression, and the Law of Nations* (Leiden, Netherlands: Martinus Nijhoff Publishers, 1998), 118.

p. 65, "Muslim children are . . ." James L. Conyers and Andrew P. Smallwood, *Malcolm X: A Historical Reader* (Durham, N.C.: Carolina Academic Press, 2008), 301.

p. 65, "[W]e don't have . . ." Adam Joel Banks, *Race, Rhetoric, and Technology: Searching for Higher Ground* (Hillsdale, N.J.: Lawrence Erlbaum Associates, 2005), 54.

p. 66, "minus the little . . ." Ibid.

p. 66, "counseling patience and . . ." Herbert Shapiro, *White Violence and Black Response: From Reconstruction to Montgomery* (Amherst: University of Massachusetts Press, 1988), 469.

p. 67, "something chemical happened . . ." Haley, *The Autobiography of Malcolm X*, 240.

p. 68, "NAACP opposes and . . ." Shapiro, *White Violence and Black Response*, 465.

p. 68, "run by a . . ." Ibid., 466.

p. 68, "twentieth century Uncle . . ." Ibid.

p. 68, "Mr. Muhammad may . . ." Christopher Alan Bracey, *Saviors or Sellouts: The Promise and Peril of Black Conservatism, from Booker T. Washington to Condoleezza Rice* (Boston: Beacon Press, 2008), 78.

p. 71,   "the torch has . . ." "John F. Kennedy," Bartleby.com, http://www.
           bartleby.com/124/pres56.html.

p. 74,   "The Honorable Elijah . . ." "Black Man's History,"
           AfricanWithin.com, http://www.africawithin.com/malcolmx/
           black_man.htm.

p. 75,   "Seven Muslims were . . ." "'And This Happened in Los Angeles,'"
           History Matters, http://historymatters.gmu.edu/d/7041.

p. 76,   "real men don't . . ." "Children's Crusade," Martin Luther King, Jr.
           Research and Education Institute, http://mlk-kpp01.stanford.edu/
           index.php/encyclopedia/encyclopedia/enc_childrens_crusade.

p. 76,   "I can't turn . . ." Haley, *The Autobiography of Malcolm X*, 270.

p. 76,   "An integrated cup . . ." "The Black Revolution," malcolm-x.org,
           http://www.malcolm-x.org/speeches/spc_06__63.htm.

p. 78,   "[T]here is plenty . . ." "The Playboy Interview," malcolm-x.org,
           http://www.malcolm-x.org/docs/int_playb.htm.

p. 78,   "The white man . . ." Ibid.

p. 79,   "Farce on Washington . . ." Haley, *The Autobiography of Malcolm
           X*, 281.

p. 79,   "picnic . . ." Ibid., 280.

p. 79,   "I observed that . . ." Ibid., 280–281.

Chapter Six: The Transformation

p. 81,   "Without a second . . ." Haley, *The Autobiography of Malcolm X*,
           301.

p. 82,   "Did you see . . ." Ibid.

p. 83,   "If you knew . . ." Ibid., 303.

p. 83,   "And then I . . ." Ibid.

p. 84,   "I learned from . . ." Ibid., 297.

p. 84,   "When you read . . ." Ibid., 299.

p. 85,   "I don't worry . . ." "Malcolm X: I Have No Fear Whatsoever
           of Anybody or Anything," YouTube, http://www.youtube.com/
           watch? v=i16OMrwxsm8&feature=relate.

p. 85,   "I shook up . . ." Les Krantz, *Ali in Action: The Man, The Moves,
           The Mouth* (Guilford, Conn: The Lyons Press, 2008), 31.

p. 86,   "gone as far . . ." George Breitman, ed., *Malcolm X Speaks: Selected
           Speeches and Statements* (Grove Press, 1965), 18.

p. 86,   "the best solution . . ." Ibid., 19.

p. 87,   "It will be . . ." Sondra K. Wilson, *Meet Me at the Theresa: The
           Story of Harlem's Most Famous Hotel* (New York: Simon & Schuster,
           2004), 229.

p. 87,   "We must find . . ." "A Declaration of Independence,"
           TeachingAmericanHistory.org, http://teachingamericanhistory.
           org/library/index.asp?document=1148.

p. 89,   "when all of . . ." Breitman, *Malcolm X Speaks*, 25.

p. 90,   "When you take . . ." Ibid., 35.

p. 90,   "[W]hen white people . . ." Ibid., 26.

p. 90,   "You let that . . ." Ibid., 42.

p. 90,   "Civil rights keeps . . ." Ibid., 35.

SOURCES CONTINUED

p. 91,   "get a rifle . . ." Josh Gottheimer, *Ripples of Hope: Great American Civil Rights Speeches* (New York: Basic Civitas Books, 2003), 256.

p. 91,   "Lyndon B. Johnson . . ." Ibid., 257.

p. 92,   "Never have I . . ." Haley, *The Autobiography of Malcolm X*, 339.

p. 92,   "There were tens . . ." Ibid., 340.

p. 93,   "[O]n this pilgrimage . . ." Ibid.

p. 93,   "Do we correctly . . ." Haley, *The Autobiography of Malcolm X*, 413.

p. 94,   "devise original educational . . ." William L. Van Deburg, *Modern Black Nationalism: From Marcus Garvey to Louis Farrakhan* (New York: New York University Press, 1997), 111.

p. 97,   "We Afro-Americans feel . . ." "Program of the Organization of Afro-American Unity," malcolm-x.org, http://www.malcolm-x.org/docs/gen_oaau.htm.

p. 97,   "I didn't come . . ." Herb Boyd, *We Shall Overcome* (Naperville, Ill.: Sourcebooks, 2004), 192.

Chapter Seven: The Assassination

p. 100,   "My house was . . ." Haley, *The Autobiography of Malcolm X*, 428.

p. 100,   "With these hypocrites . . ." Mattias Gardell, *In the Name of Elijah Muhammad: Louis Farrakhan and the Nation of Islam* (Durham, N.C.: Duke University Press, 1996), 82.

p. 100,   "such a man . . ." Ibid.

p. 100,   "Why are they . . ." "Malcolm X: I Have No Fear Whatsoever of Anybody or Anything," YouTube, http://www.youtube.com/watch? v=i16OMrwxsm8&feature=relate.

p. 101,   "I have been . . ." Haley, *The Autobiography of Malcolm X*, 428

p. 102,   "Well, I've lived . . ." "Interview with Gordon Parks," malcolm-x. org, http://www.malcolm-x.org/docs/int_parks.htm.

p. 102,   "The sickness and . . ." Ibid.

p. 103,   "Wake up, brother . . ." Haley, *The Autobiography of Malcolm X*, 431.

p. 103,   "*Asalaikum*, brothers and . . ." Ibid., 434.

p. 103,   "Take your hand . . ." Ibid.

p. 104,   "They're killing my . . ." Ibid., 435.

p. 105,   "Dear Daddy, I . . ." Russell J. Rickford, *Betty Shabazz, Surviving Malcolm X* (Naperville, Ill.: Sourcebooks, 2005), 237.

p. 105,   "Malcolm died according . . ." Haley, *The Autobiography of Malcolm X*, 440.

p. 105,   "our own black . . ." "Eulogy for Malcolm X," Hartford Web Publishing, http://www.hartford-hwp.com/archives/45a/071.html.

p. 105,   "They will say . . ." Ibid.

pp. 105, 107, "While we did . . ." "A Common Solution," The Martin Luther King, Jr. Research and Education Institute, http://mlk-kpp01.stanford.edu/kingweb/additional_resources/articles/common_solution.htm.

p. 109,   "such a man . . ." Michael Wilson, "For Malcolm X's Grandson, a Clouded Path," *New York Times*, September 6, 2003. http://www.nytimes.com/2003/09/06/nyregion/for-malcolm-x-s-grandson-a-clouded-path.html?pagewanted=all&src=pm.

p. 109,   "Of course, yes . . ." Charisse Jones, "Qubilah Shabazz: An 'Ideal Young Lady,'" *New York Times*, January 13, 1995, http://www.nytimes.com/1995/01/13/us/qubilah-shabazz-an-ideal-young-lady.html.

p. 109,   "I may have . . ." "Farrakhan Admission On Malcolm X," CBSNews.com, February 11, 2009, http://www.cbsnews.com/stories/2000/05/10/60minutes/main194051.shtml.

p. 110,   "I was struck . . ." Wilson, "For Malcolm X's Grandson, a Clouded Path."

Chapter Eight: The Legacy of Malcolm X

p. 113,   "The Negroes of . . ." James Baldwin, *The Price of the Ticket: Collected Nonfiction, 1948–1985* (New York: Macmillan, 1985), 371.

p. 114,   "We didn't land . . ." "Malcolm X: We Are Africans Who Were Kidnapped and Brought to America," YouTube, http://www.youtube.com/watch? v=xDXPpfGAZrU.

p. 114,   "I see America . . ." "Malcolm X Speaks," AfricaWithin.com, http://www.africawithin.com/malcolmx/malcolm_speaks.htm.

p. 114,   "[S]omehow that book . . ." David Bradley, "Malcolm's Mythmaking," *Transition* (56), 34–35.

p. 114,   "More than any . . ." "Document History of the Modern Civil Rights Movement, The African American Experience," http://testaae.greenwood.com/doc_print.aspx?fileID=LMR&chapterID=LMR- 1141&path=books/greenwood.

p. 115,   "By any means . . ." "By Any Means Necessary," YouTube, http://www.youtube.com/watch?v=M4DlfEQ7cyk.

p. 115,   "If America don't . . ." "The Cambridge Convergence," The Martin Luther King, Jr. Research and Education Institute, http://mlk-kpp01.stanford.edu/index.php/home/pages?page=http://mlk-kpp01.stanford.edu/kingweb/about_the_project/ccarson/articles/cambridge_convergence.htm.

p. 115,   "We been saying . . ." Cleveland Sellers and Robert L. Terrell, *The River of No Return: The Autobiography of a Black Militant and the Life and Death of SNCC* (Jackson: University of Mississippi Press, 1990), 166.

p. 116,   "Malcolm had a . . ." Stokely Carmichael and Michael Thelwell, *Ready for Revolution: The Life and Struggles of Stokely Carmichael (Kwame Ture)* (New York: Simon & Schuster, 2003), 259.

p. 117,   "I threw about . . ." Bobby Seale, *Seize the Time: The Story of the Black Panther Party and Huey P. Newton* (Baltimore: Black Classic Press, 1991), 3.

SOURCES CONTINUED

p. 117,   "Eldridge says Malcolm . . ." Ibid.

p. 117,   "the Black Panther . . ." Huey P. Newton, *Revolutionary Suicide* (New York: Penguin, 2009), Google eBook.

p. 119,   "We want freedom . . ." Philip S. Foner, ed., *The Black Panthers Speak* (Cambridge, Mass.: Da Capo Press, 2002), 2.

p. 120,   "Hey, after a . . ." Carmichael and Thelwell, *Ready for Revolution*, 440.

p. 120,   "As a minority . . ." Author interview, September 27, 2011.

p. 121,   "Only Malcolm X's . . ." Barack Obama, *Dreams from My Father: A Story of Race and Inheritance* (New York: Random House Digital, 2007), 86.

p. 121,   "students of diverse . . ." "Mission Document," Malcolm X College, http://malcolmx.ccc.edu/About_MXC/mission.asp.

p. 122,   "Too black, too . . ." Marcus Reeves, *Somebody Scream!: Rap Music's Rise to Prominence in the Aftershock of Black Power* (New York: Macmillan, 2009), 72.

p. 122,   "Dozens of prominent . . ." "Malcolm X Project," Center for Contemporary Black History, http://www.columbia.edu/cu/ccbh/html/ccbh_proj_mxp.html.

p. 122,   "a hero for . . ." Manning Marable, *Malcolm X: A Life of Reinvention* (New York: Penguin, 2011), Google eBook.

p. 123,   "What's next? Malcolm . . ." Mike Littwin, "Malcolm X Story Deserves Dignity, Not Designer Wear," *The Baltimore Sun*, November 18, 1992, http://articles.baltimoresun.com/1992-11-18/features/1992323060_1_malcolm-x- spike-lee-black.

p. 123,   "people as unlikely . . ." David Remnick, "This American Life," *New Yorker*, April 25, 2011, http://www.newyorker.com/arts/critics/books/2011/04/25/110425crbo_books_remnick.

BIBLIOGRAPHY

"'And This Happened in Los Angeles.'" History Matters. http://historymatters.gmu.edu/d/7041.

Baldwin, James. *The Price of the Ticket: Collected Nonfiction, 1948–1985.* New York: Macmillan, 1985.

Banks, Adam Joel. *Race, Rhetoric, and Technology: Searching for Higher Ground.* Hillsdale, N.J.: Lawrence Erlbaum Associates, 2005.

"Black Man's History." AfricanWithin.com. http://www.africawithin.com/malcolmx/black_man.htm.

"The Black Revolution." malcolm-x.org. http://www.malcolm-x.org/speeches/spc_06__63.htm.

Boyd, Herb. *We Shall Overcome.* Naperville, Ill.: Sourcebooks, 2004.

Bracey, Christopher Alan. *Saviors or Sellouts: The Promise and Peril of Black Conservatism, from Booker T. Washington to Condoleezza Rice.* Boston: Beacon Press, 2008.

Bradley, David. "Malcolm's Mythmaking." *Transition* (56).

Breitman, George, ed. *Malcolm X Speaks: Selected Speeches and Statements.* Grove Press, 1965.

"By Any Means Necessary." YouTube. http://www.youtube.com/watch?v=M4DlfEQ7cyk.

"The Cambridge Convergence." The Martin Luther King, Jr. Research and Education Institute. http://mlk-kpp01.stanford.edu/index.php/home/pages?page=http://mlk-kpp01.stanford.edu/kingweb/about_the_project/ccarson/articles/cambridge_convergence.htm.

Carmichael, Stokely, and Michael Thelwell. *Ready for Revolution: The Life and Struggles of Stokely Carmichael (Kwame Ture).* New York: Simon & Schuster, 2003.

Carson, Clayborne, primary consultant. *Civil Rights Chronicle: The African-American Struggle for Freedom.* Lincolnwood, Ill.: Legacy Publishing, 2003.

"Children's Crusade." Martin Luther King, Jr. Research and Education Institute. http://mlk-kpp01.stanford.edu/index.php/encyclopedia/encyclopedia/enc_childrens_crusade.

Cole, Karen S. "Sister Betty X Shabazz." Ezine Articles. http://ezinearticles.com/?Sister-Betty-X-Shabazz&id=613236.

"A Common Solution." The Martin Luther King, Jr. Research and Education Institute. http://mlk-kpp01.stanford.edu/kingweb/additional_resources/articles/common_solution.htm.

Conyers, James L., and Andrew P. Smallwood. *Malcolm X: A Historical Reader.* Durham, N.C.: Carolina Academic Press, 2008.

"A Declaration of Independence." TeachingAmericanHistory.org. http://teachingamericanhistory.org/library/index.asp?document=1148.

"Document History of the Modern Civil Rights Movement. The African American Experience." http://testaae.greenwood.com/doc_print.aspx?fileID=LMR&chapterID=LMR-1141&path=books/greenwood.

"Eulogy for Malcolm X." Hartford Web Publishing. http://www.hartford-hwp.com/archives/45a/071.html.

"Farrakhan Admission On Malcolm X." CBSNews.com, February 11, 2009. http://www.cbsnews.com/stories/2000/05/10/60minutes/main194051.shtml.

Foner, Philip S., ed. *The Black Panthers Speak.* Cambridge, Mass.: Da Capo Press, 2002.

Gardell, Mattias. *In the Name of Elijah Muhammad: Louis Farrakhan and the Nation of Islam.* Durham, N.C.: Duke University Press, 1996.

Gottheimer, Josh. *Ripples of Hope: Great American Civil Rights Speeches.* New York: Basic Civitas Books, 2003.

Haley, Alex, and Malcolm X. *The Autobiography of Malcolm X.* New York: Ballantine Books, 1990.

Hebel, Udo J., and Christoph Wagner. *Pictorial Cultures and Political Iconographies: Approaches, Perspectives, Case Studies from Europe and America.* Berlin: De Gruyter, 2011.

"The I Have a Dream Speech." U.S. Constitution Online. http://www.usconstitution.net/dream.html.

"Interview with Gordon Parks." malcolm-x.org. http://www.malcolm-x.org/docs/int_parks.htm.

Jacques Garvey, Amy. *The Philosophy and Opinions of Marcus Garvey: Or, Africa for the Africans.* Dover, Mass.: The Majority Press, 1986.

"John F. Kennedy." Bartleby.com. http://www.bartleby.com/124/pres56.html.

Jones, Charisse. "Qubilah Shabazz: An 'Ideal Young Lady,'" *New York Times*, January 13, 1995. http://www.nytimes.com/1995/01/13/us/qubilah-shabazz-an-ideal-young-lady.html.

Jones, Thomas David. *Human Rights: Group Defamation, Freedom of Expression, and the Law of Nations.* Leiden, Netherlands: Martinus Nijhoff Publishers, 1998.

Krantz, Les. *Ali in Action: The Man, The Moves, The Mouth.* Guilford, Conn: The Lyons Press, 2008.

Littwin, Mike. "Malcolm X Story Deserves Dignity, Not Designer Wear." *Baltimore Sun*, November 18, 1992. http://articles.baltimoresun.com/1992-11-18/features/1992323060_1_malcolm-x-spike-lee-black.

"Malcolm X Project." Center for Contemporary Black History. http://www.columbia.edu/cu/ccbh/html/ccbh_proj_mxp.html.

"Malcolm X Quotes." Malcolm X Online. http://www.malcolmxonline.com/malcolm-x-quotes.html.

"Malcolm X Speaks." AfricaWithin.com. http://www.africawithin.com/malcolmx/malcolm_speaks.htm.

"Malcolm X: I Have No Fear Whatsoever of Anybody or Anything." YouTube. http://www.youtube.com/watch?v=i16OMrwxsm8&feature=relate.

"Malcolm X: We Are Africans Who Were Kidnapped and Brought to America." YouTube. http://www.youtube.com/watch?v=xDXPpfGAZrU.

"Malcolm X: Who Taught You to Hate Yourself?" YouTube. http://www.youtube.com/watch?v=gRSgUTWffMQ.

"Malcolmology 101, #7: Johnson X Hinton." Malcolm X: A Life of Reinvention, http://www.malcolmxbio.com/node/15.

———, #13: Fidel Castro in Harlem." Malcolm X: A Life of Reinvention. http://www.malcolmxbio.com/node/24.

Marable, Manning. *Malcolm X: A Life of Reinvention.* New York: Penguin, 2011.

"Mission Document." Malcolm X College. http://malcolmx.ccc.edu/About_MXC/mission.asp.

Newton, Huey P. *Revolutionary Suicide.* New York: Penguin, 2009.

Obama, Barack. *Dreams from My Father: A Story of Race and Inheritance.* New York: Random House Digital, 2007.

"The Playboy Interview." malcolm-x.org. http://www.malcolm-x.org/docs/int_playb.htm.

"Program of the Organization of Afro-American Unity." malcolm-x.org. http://www.malcolm-x.org/docs/gen_oaau.htm.

Reeves, Marcus. *Somebody Scream!: Rap Music's Rise to Prominence in the Aftershock of Black Power.* New York: Macmillan, 2009.

Remnick, David. "This American Life." *The New Yorker*, April 25, 2011. http://www.newyorker.com/arts/critics/books/2011/04/25/110425crbo_books_remnick.

Rickford, Russell J. *Betty Shabazz, Surviving Malcolm X*. Naperville, Ill.: Sourcebooks, 2005.

Seale, Bobby. *Seize the Time: The Story of the Black Panther Party and Huey P. Newton*. Baltimore: Black Classic Press, 1991.

Sellers, Cleveland, and Robert L. Terrell. *The River of No Return: The Autobiography of a Black Militant and the Life and Death of SNCC*. Jackson: University of Mississippi Press, 1990.

Shapiro, Herbert. *White Violence and Black Response: From Reconstruction to Montgomery*. Amherst: University of Massachusetts Press, 1988.

Van Deburg, William L. *Modern Black Nationalism: From Marcus Garvey to Louis Farrakhan*. New York: New York University Press, 1997.

Wilson, Michael. "For Malcolm X's Grandson, a Clouded Path." *New York Times*, September 6, 2003. http://www.nytimes.com/2003/09/06/nyregion/for-malcolm-x-s-grandson-a-clouded-path.html?pagewanted=all&src=pm.

Wilson, Sondra K. *Meet Me at the Theresa: The Story of Harlem's Most Famous Hotel*. New York: Simon & Schuster, 2004.

WEB SITES

The Malcolm X Project at Columbia University
http://www.columbia.edu/cu/ccbh/mxp/index.html
This site features a biography of Malcolm X, photo gallery, timeline, list of resources, and interviews with friends and family of Malcolm.

American Experience: Marcus Garvey: Look for Me in the Whirlwind
http://www.pbs.org/wgbh/amex/garvey/index.html
This American Experience site explores the influential black nationalist leader Marcus Garvey, who influenced Malcolm's parents.

P.O.V.: Brother Outsider: The Life of Bayard Rustin
http://www.pbs.org/pov/pov2002/brotheroutsider/
Listen to a 1962 debate on integration and separation featuring Malcolm X and Bayard Rustin, the subject of this PBS P.O.V. Web site (the debate is in the "Rustin's Work" section of the site).

Amy Goodman of Democracy Now Interviews Manning Marable
http: //www.democracynow.org/article pl?sid=05
/02/2/1458213&mode=thread&tid=25
Manning Marable talks about new information on Malcolm's assassination, his plans to unite the civil rights and black nationalist movements, and the three missing chapters from his autobiography.

INDEX

Ali, John, 100
Ali, Muhammad, 57, 85–86, *86*

Baldwin, James, 113
Black Muslim movement, 86, 100–102
Black Panthers, 96, 109, 117, *118,* 119
Black Power movement, 16, 115–117, 119
black supremacy, 59, 65–67
Brown, H. Rap, 115, *115*
Brown v. Board of Education, 59, *59*
Butler, Norman 3X, 108

Carmichael, Stokely, 109, 115–117, *115*
Castro, Fidel, 72–73, *73*
Civil Rights Bill, 87, 89
civil rights movement, 12, 59, 67–68, 71, 76, 87, 89–90, 96–97,
    113, 120
Cleaver, Eldridge, 117
Congressional Black Caucus, 116
Congress of Racial Equality (CORE), 89–90

Davis, Ossie, 105

Fard, Wallace, 46, *52*
Farrakhan, Louis, *56–57,* 57, 65, 100, 109–110
Freedom Rides, 72
Freedom Summer, 72, 94, 97
Fruit of Islam, 53, 62, 73, 107–108

Garvey, Marcus, 19, 22, *23,* 24

Haley, Alex, 78, 93, 102, 107
Hampton, Fred, 109
hate, concept of, 11–13, 68, 81, 105
Hayer, Talmadge, 104, 107–109
Hinton, Johnson X, 62–63
Hoover, J. Edgar, 108–109, *108*
human rights, 93–95

PHOTO CREDITS

All images used in this book that are not in the public domain are credited
in the listing that follows: